About th

Born and brought up in Yorkshire, educated in Scotland, Catharine also lived in Cambridge and London before moving to Lusaka, Zambia. She is a fully qualified accountant, married with two children and currently lives near Manchester.

ISBN-13 978 1482316339
ISBN-10 1482316331

Copyright © Catharine Withenay 2013

All rights reserved.
No part of this publication may be reproduced, stored in a retrieval system or transmitted, in any form or by any means, without the prior written permission of the author, nor be otherwise circulated in any form of binding or cover other than that in which it is published and without a similar condition being imposed on the purchaser.

www.catharinewithenay.com

William Shakespeare quote from Henry IV Part I, Act I, Scene 2

Disclaimer

My father once told me,
"Never let the truth get in the way of a good story."

Some facts have been twisted to make a story. Some names have been changed. That, I'm afraid, is a writer's prerogative.

Nevertheless, this story is based upon truth, although the words are mine alone. Even the words I have written that others have spoken are my interpretation, not necessarily precise memories, and so should in no way be taken as an exact representation of others' views or opinions.

We left the UK in June 2003 to live in Lusaka, Zambia. Many things have changed since then, in both countries, not least of which is that you can't now check your luggage in ahead of time at Paddington for flights from Heathrow. I fear we may have helped the authorities make that decision.

Cover design by designforwriters.com

IN THE SHADE OF THE MULBERRY TREE

A year in Zambia

Catharine Withenay

ACKNOWLEDGEMENTS

I owe a huge debt of gratitude to many people who have helped, tweaked and cajoled this book into existence. Without them I would still be floundering in front of a blank screen, willing the stories to write themselves.

For constructive criticism I have benefitted from the combined wisdom of the WEA NorthEast Creative Writers' Group, Poynton Writers' Guild and the editorial comments of Caroline Smailes, Catherine Lain and Shelley Weiner.

My thanks go to Neil and Nathalie Marshall, who brainstormed the title over ice-creams after a long walk, and have been unwavering in their support. Thanks also to Ann Bennett for proofreading so perfectly pedantically.

My friends in Zambia combined to make a year (and more) of my life most magical and special. Their representation here is constructed entirely from my memories and I trust I have done none of them a disservice. For this book I particularly thank Andrew, Daniel, David, Eckhard, Fortune, Gwyn, Kelly, Joan, Leah, Maggie, Margriet, Natalie, Paul, Bishop Paul, Precious, Rachel, Richie, Sherry, Tanvir and Winnie.

Above all, my thanks goes to the most patient and tolerant supporters of my writing: my father, my children and, most of all, my husband. They have provided both the fodder and the space to write about it, correcting my errors with tact and making me endless cups of tea. They are owed more than a few words here could ever express.

*For Stephen, Matthew and Eleanor,
without whom none of this would have been possible.*

Here we go round the mulberry bush,
   the mulberry bush, the mulberry bush,
Here we go round the mulberry bush
   on a cold and frosty morning.

Children's rhyme

PASSPORT PANDEMONIUM

It was as the Heathrow Express was dipping underground, leaving London and all that I knew behind, that calamity struck.

"Stephen, where are the passports?"

He stood up to check. They weren't in his coat pocket. They weren't in his rucksack. They weren't even in the basket under the pram where we put everything else.

They were nowhere to be found.

We were still searching when the train pulled into the airport. I knew with a cold certainty that they were lost.

It wasn't as if I had even wanted to emigrate. It had been a year since Stephen received the funding to do his medical research: anything to do with childhood malnutrition, dendritic cells or the immune system and he was in his element. We had both known the project meant living abroad for a couple of years, but I'd secretly hoped that something might stop this happening. What did Zambia hold for me? What if the children caught malaria? How would we cope far from family and friends?

Still, I didn't plan for us to lose our passports an hour before departure.

We hurried from the train to find a representative from the airline.

"Can we fly without them?" Even as I asked I knew it was a ridiculous question.

The woman smiled patiently. "No." Apparently overseas travel demands a passport.

"Did we leave them on the desk when checking in our luggage at Paddington?" I enquired. "Could you phone through and ask?"

No-one had seen them.

"You should empty your bags and double-check," she said.

I eyed her with disdain. She may have been right, but she didn't have a toddler and a baby to entertain at the same time. Nor would she be unpacking four bulging bags prepared for a family's emigration to Africa plus everything necessary to survive a ten-hour flight with my children.

There was no choice. I turned and found a space on the floor in front of the desk. I emptied everything. No sign of the passports anywhere.

Stephen left to find a phone and call anyone who might have seen them. After checking in at lunchtime we had spent a wonderful afternoon in the early summer sunshine in Hyde Park with friends before catching the train here. Perhaps they would know, or be able to look at Paddington?

Eleanor got grizzly in the pram so I took her out and bounced her up and down a bit. I scoured the hand luggage once more. Could they be caught in between the nappies? No. Inside a book? No.

It dawned on me that Eleanor was hungry. I had no choice but to leave Matthew to his own devices and, sighing, sit cross-legged on the cold floor. In the same way as I'd felt about the indignities of childbirth, I was past caring how I looked: I just wanted the passports back. I just wanted to get on that aeroplane and get this African experience over and done with.

Matthew was experimenting with the trolleys: pushing, climbing, over, under – and the airport officials were frowning. One marched over to tell me that I must not allow my son to play on the trolleys, pointing out the sign on a pillar behind her.

"Matthew, come here," I called half-heartedly. At two-and-a-half, he was toddling around the barriers in his own make-believe world. I couldn't do anything much with him while feeding Eleanor so turned my back to both the poster and the official, and left him to his private game.

I was alone, too bewildered even to cry.

☙

I glanced around the busy terminal. It had been a glorious English summer's day and everyone seemed light-hearted and excited. I shifted awkwardly, trying to ease the pain of the unforgiving floor while cradling my hungry daughter. Physically, a slightly more comfortable position; mentally, still sitting on a bed of nails. The airline was holding the plane for us. Guilt flooded my brain as I thought of the other passengers cursing their flight's late departure. I wondered what explanation the airline gave. *"I'm sorry, ladies and gentlemen. There will be a slight delay to the departure of your flight to Lusaka this evening while the Withenay family locate their passports."*

Stephen returned.

"Any news?"

He shook his head. "Nothing. I've tried lost property and the police – nothing. Our parents haven't heard anything either. They're quite upset, but what can they do? I've also tried..."

His mobile rang. It was our friends from the afternoon calling from Paddington. "Yes...yes..." I was hopeful as I listened to half the conversation. "Ah well, never mind. Thank you for looking."

Stephen's drawn face said it all.

Glancing down I realised Eleanor had finished feeding and fallen asleep. Carefully I placed her in the pram. I called to Matthew and together we began to put everything back in the bags, still rifling through every magazine and opening each zipped pocket in the vain hope of finding four passports. He wasn't much help but at least it kept him away from the trolleys and the woman with the frown.

The customer relations manager from the airline came over.

"Have you found them?"

I was on my knees and paused to look at him. *Does it look like we've found them?*

"We've held the plane back for as long as we can. Do you know where they are?"

Do I know where they are? Do you think I'd be crawling around on this dirty concrete floor, with all my belongings exposed, if I knew where the passports were?

My husband was more polite than I would have been. He gently apologised but no, we couldn't find the passports.

They couldn't hold the flight any longer: we had to admit defeat. The gentleman walked away speaking into his walkie-talkie as our luggage, so efficiently checked in at Paddington six hours ago, was taken off the plane.

Only then did I crumple and cry.

≈

The children fell asleep quickly and easily. Stephen had been back and forth to the terminal to collect our luggage which dominated the other side of our hotel room: three large suitcases, two rucksacks, a pram and a travel cot. I broke into the mini-bar for a drink, reasoning that at times like this the hotel prices were irrelevant, while Stephen kept himself busy moving cases around: anything to avoid stopping and really considering the situation.

"Where are they?" I asked feebly. It was a pointless question, I knew. We'd picked over the day with a toothcomb again and again.

"I don't know." Stephen stopped and sat down heavily on the bed. "I don't know," he repeated.

There was silence.

"We had them to check in," I said.

"The woman at the counter gave them back to me," said Stephen. "And then what happened?"

"Matthew's nappy exploded." My eyes opened wide as I recollected this incident, mirrored by Stephen's as the memory rushed back.

"Oh, yes – we had to change him quickly."

"You just did it right there and then, just beside the check-in counters. I pushed Eleanor around in the pram a bit to keep her quiet while you did the nappy. I remember putting the luggage trolley back with the others – oh my goodness!" I gasped, putting my hand to my mouth, "Were they there? Were they in that tray part by the handle?"

Stephen looked at me. "I'm almost willing that to be true, but I had them. I don't remember handing them

In the shade of the mulberry tree

to you. Did I just leave them on the ground when I'd cleaned Matthew up?"

"It's possible, but wouldn't we have seen them as we were leaving? I'm certain the floor was clear."

"And surely someone would have handed them in, maybe at the check-in desk or at lost property, or even the police? I've tried them all – nothing! There were nearly five hours before we discovered they were missing, plenty of time for them to be handed in." Stephen sighed.

We sank back into silence, each lost in our own misery, each trying to work out what had happened, each trying not to blame the other.

And my mind ran through the practicalities. New passports. A trip to Petty France. A fast-track system, and we had all our documents in one of the suitcases over by the window. I perked up at the thought. "It shouldn't be too difficult to get replacement passports," I said brightly. "An early start, some queuing, but we've got copies of all our documents with us so it should be straightforward."

A final exhausted calm fell upon me as I anticipated the next day. Others had done this before us: it's not difficult, just expensive. Sleep beckoned. I didn't think it could get worse.

༄

"I beg your pardon?"

"I was born in Canada."

"Yes, I know that. What I don't get is how it affects your passport. Surely you are just renewing the old one?" I said. To me, it was simple.

"Ah, yes, well, you would think so. But from what the woman said on the phone, because I have a Canadian birth certificate, I need to have more evidence of British citizenship. I need Dad's certificate as well to get a new passport."

"But having got that, it's straightforward?"

Stephen shuffled awkwardly. "Erm…yes, but she said that cases like mine take at least a week."

"A week! What are we going to do for a week? We can't stay here. Oh good grief!"

My head dropped to my hands as I tried to work out how to pull it all together. Stephen had been on and off the phone from early morning and we had until midday – little more than an hour – to check out. We needed to be in London to get the new passports, but our house was rented out and none of our friends had room for all four of us (and three large suitcases, two rucksacks, a pram and a travel cot). Where should we go? My Dad's? Stephen's parents? Neither lived close by. We were stranded in no-man's-land.

Stephen sat down beside me and gently rubbed my back. "It'll be all right," he said. I looked up through my fingers at his warm, loving face. In my heart I knew it to be true. What is a week's delay in the grand scheme of things? But in my emotional state it was a lifetime.

"All done!" Matthew declared, pointing at his completed jigsaw.

"Well done, boy! Now, do you want to do it again?" Joyfully he broke up the pieces and repeated the puzzle. I turned back to my conversation with Stephen.

"You'd better go and sort out the paperwork from the police, officially report the passports as lost. Ellie's asleep, so one of us has to stay here. I can be a point of contact should anything happen."

"OK. I'll call if there's any news," he said.

"Just be back before twelve – I can't check out with all this by myself."

I returned to Matthew and his puzzle, grateful for the innocence of childhood, untouched by the whirlwind blowing round my head. How do we get the replacement passports? What about the flight: are we now facing the price of another long-haul flight to Zambia in a couple of weeks' time, or longer? The costs are mounting up and midday fast approaches. Do we stay another night?

I tried to entertain Matthew in the hotel room without causing any damage. He discovered that his toy car, with a little help, could fly spectacularly off the end of the bed. After a precarious moment with a glass of water and a TV screen, I persuaded him to have another go at the jigsaw puzzle. Reluctantly he agreed.

At 11.30 the phone rang.

"Is that Mrs Withenay?" asked a woman with a Jamaican accent.

"Ye-es," I replied warily.

"It's Lost Property at Paddington," she said. I held my breath. "We have your passports here."

"Oh!" I gasped. I didn't know what to say. "Fantastic! Oh! Thank you! If you were here I'd give you a great big kiss! Thank you!"

I sensed she was grateful that several miles separated us. "Yes, yes, well, that's as may be. Anyway, there's four of them. I'll put them all in one envelope so you just have to pay one fee to collect them."

"Oh, thank you! Thank you!"

I cried tears of relief then whooped with joy. Matthew looked up, bemused.

"We're on our way, Matthew. We're on our way."

❦

Two days later we caught the next available flight. This time we checked in at the airport with three hours to spare. This time we sat in the coffee bar and watched the planes come and go. This time we waited, entertaining our impatient children by walking up and down the departure lounge before the overnight flight.

This time I had the passports. In my bag, for definite. I know: I checked.

This time we made it to Zambia, to my new life under African skies.

SHADOWS

We took a sharp left-turn through a gap in the hedge, missed the ditch, and pulled up in front of a wall. Its eight-foot height shielded the mystery beyond, a solid block of white paint blinding in the sunlight.

We were here.

This was what I was to call home.

After the trauma of the previous few days I should have felt relief that we had finally made it. Instead I was full of trepidation, afraid of what I'd let myself in for. A gate in an archway led through to the garden, a square of scratchy grass dominated by a giant mulberry tree. Its shadow stretched over everything, touching the one-storey building and waving at the car on the other side of the wall.

Stephen found a key on the jumbled bunch that worked in the front door. Opening it revealed a large, gloomy room. The dark brown concrete floor sucked out the light and the air was stifling and stale. It had the musty smell of longstanding vacancy mixed with the sharpness of fresh paint. It felt unloved: empty, echoing and bleak. It did nothing to lift my mood.

Our footsteps echoed across the floor. I was silent, overwhelmed by the journey to get here. I held my eight-month-old daughter tight to my hip, seemingly my sole ally in this strange world. Clutching each other we'd survived the drive from the airport, bouncing along in the back of a battered old Land Rover. While my husband, Stephen, sat up front chatting to the driver, we had been squashed in the back between the pram and luggage on one side and my two-year-old son on the other. There were no seatbelts, no car seats for the children and the luggage was stacked behind, open to the elements. In the odd moments when I wasn't fearful for my children's lives I had wondered what would happen if it rained, if there was a quick shower or a tropical storm.

Matthew skidded across the shiny floor. "Whee!" he squealed in glee, oblivious to my fears in moving to this new place.

Stephen was talking quickly, a nervous reaction to compensate for my silence. He kept glancing at me for approval. "This is the living room – oh good, they've fixed the mosquito netting – and through there is the dining room and then the kitchen. This way...is to the bedrooms. Oh!" He stopped short at the first door. "No mattress here. Hmm."

I followed quietly, trying to take it all in. I knew he'd done his best to prepare the way for me but I still didn't want to be here. After the exploits of our journey, my slight hope that we wouldn't make it had hit reality. I had to view this positively or I would go under. But my first impression was negative, walking on cold concrete floors, looking at vast concrete wardrobes and shivering in their shadows.

At the end of a long corridor was the bathroom. I took a deep breath. No sparkling chrome, no pristine white bath, no toilet paper. The basin was cracked, the bathtub was yellowing, the shower attachment had perished and the ageing mirror looked like it could fall off the wall at any moment. Its gloom matched my mood, and I wondered how I would manage any of my bodily functions in there.

A peek into one of the other bedrooms revealed both the missing mattresses: one double mattress (torn) and one single mattress. "Could we sleep here tonight, as planned?" Stephen asked. What about mosquito nets? Bedding? Food?

I returned to the main living area and tried the kitchen. It was small with just enough room to turn around. Estate agents' brochures would describe it as 'fitted', although I found the pebbled concrete work surfaces and metal cupboard doors held no warmth. It felt like I was going to live in a box of rocks. There was a space for a fridge and a cooker, exposed wires lying loose on the floor, and an open fuse box glared at me from the remaining wall. Upmarket décor this was never going to be, and it was a far cry from my cosy terraced house in London.

I ventured back outside to help with the suitcases. Stephen had unloaded all the luggage from the Land Rover and was prattling on about the house. I hardly heard him, lost in my private world of misery. It may have been our house, but it was not our home. I looked at Eleanor, resting on my hip, oblivious to my turmoil. Her sunny face matched the weather outside and I kissed her forehead. For her, and for Matthew, I had to hold it together.

The vehicle left, and I saw my escape route vanishing in a cloud of dust and diesel fumes. What was my future now? This concrete box?

As I looked round anxiously for Matthew, a tall white man was walking up the drive towards us. Stephen greeted him warmly with a firm handshake. He turned back to me.

"Catharine, this is Richie – you remember the guy I told you about, who is living here while working for Tearfund for a year?"

I smiled as I greeted him. Stephen had stayed with Richie in the flat opposite during one of his planning visits and in so doing found our house available for rent. They were soon lost in conversation while I was trying to prevent Matthew from running off anywhere. I delved into the nappy bag to retrieve a sunhat for Eleanor and battled with Matthew to wear his (I lost).

"Would you like dinner tonight?" I overheard, together with Stephen's rapid assent. Richie looked to me for confirmation.

I juggled my tired baby from arm to arm, dropped Matthew's toy car to squeals of dismay and said, "That would be lovely. Are you sure you can cope with us?"

Richie laughed a touch uncertainly, "I'll try."

"I'm vegetarian," I added.

"Oh, no problem," he said, although the hesitation that flickered across his eyes said otherwise.

I retrieved the toy car, adjusted the muslin cloth on my shoulder and altered Eleanor's position so she rested over it. She was getting crabby and needed a feed. Soon after, Richie left, no doubt having to change his planned menu and probably wondering what he'd let himself in for. Stephen took the final suitcase and called to Matthew. Inside there were no seats, so I sat on the cold, hard floor to feed my baby and tried not to cry.

༄

It was night time and I lay in bed, frustrated at my inability to sleep. I was exhausted by the day's activities and the previous night's lack of sleep on the plane. Everything was strange. We had chosen to stay in the house, reliant on borrowed bits and pieces to see us through. Richie loaned us sheets and a grey blanket but they were thin and the mattress lay on the cold concrete floor. Richie was doing his best to be my lifesaver, whether he knew it or not. Dinner was delicious and, contrary to my first impressions, not in the slightest bit compromised by my vegetarianism. He had spoken warmly of his secondment to the Evangelical Fellowship of Zambia, or EFZ as he referred to it. Though formed as an umbrella organisation for all the evangelical churches in Zambia, the head office in Lusaka co-ordinated relief work for rural areas as well, hence the link with Tearfund. Richie's secondment was uncovering a number of gaps in the expectations of both donors and recipients. His light banter about the office characters and the slow, slow, slow pace of anything happening saved me from focusing on my own concerns, and also distracted Stephen from talking about his research. For this, I was most grateful.

I turned on the uncomfortable mattress, grateful for the warmth of my husband's body beside me. There were no curtains at the window so, although I was covered by a mosquito net, outside felt very near. The day's hustle and bustle had gone; in its place were crickets and cicadas shrilling their tunes, and the occasional frog adding a bass line. Cool air was gently wafting in through the missing windowpane, laden with a peculiar mix of dust and the damp smell of trees at night.

How had we got here? All those months of practical preparation (packing, finances and organisation) yet I was clearly unprepared for reality. I knew next to nothing about the country in which I would live for the next two years. This was the total of my knowledge: Zambia is just north of Zimbabwe – where there is trouble – and it is large. A colleague in the UK had said it was known for its copper, which came as a surprise. Was I supposed to know that sort of thing?

The conical net felt constricting and uncomfortable. Paranoia had dictated that the net be tucked in under all four sides of the mattress. I didn't want a single malaria-ridden mosquito passing through the netting, but that was easier said than done, as we also had to get into the bed in the dark after switching off the main light. How would I protect my children from mosquitoes? I wouldn't even know what one looked like unless Stephen was to show me. It was scary having to be so reliant on my sleeping husband. Why didn't I pay more attention earlier? Had I been in denial, thinking we wouldn't actually come?

Africa held no attraction for me. Why should it? My life story was so very straightforward, unadventurous, settled. Nothing had prepared me for falling in love with a doctor and moving around for the best jobs the health service could offer, nor for that man to have a particular passion for tropical medicine.

I'd tried to ignore it. There had been talk of going abroad shortly after our marriage, but this had been delayed or deferred as different work opportunities arose. Stephen spent three months working in Ghana and I'd hoped that would flush the desire out of his system. No such luck. It was fully ingrained, part of his overall raison d'être. I knew as soon as I visited him there, as he proudly showed me around the hospital. Following the return from Ghana, research grant applications began.

I should have been proud of him and his hard work to achieve the research funding. I should have been glad to have this opportunity to witness another way of life. I should have been delighted at the prospects for my children, that they would have such a chance to meet new friends, to live outside in the sun, to run around in clean, fresh air.

I should have been proud, glad and delighted. Instead I was glum, despondent and fearful. What was there here for me?

Eventually I drifted into sleep praying simply for the strength to get through the next day.

TENTATIVE STEPS

Monday morning. Stephen rustled up a mug of tea and, after a good sniff at the carton that stood on the side overnight, poured milk onto our cereal.

"I must go into the hospital," he said.

My eyes nearly popped out. "You what?"

"Go into the hospital, to work."

"You're joking, right?"

"No, I'm supposed to be working. I've got to go into the hospital."

"But we only arrived yesterday! We have to get things organised, get furniture, a fridge, blankets. No, no you can't!"

You can't leave me here on my own, I screamed internally.

"I am being paid to work," he said. "I've told them I'd be in today. I took all of last week off work. It's not meant to be a holiday, you know!"

"I know that, but surely they can't expect you in on your first full day in the country? Surely they'd understand that we need to get sorted out? I know, last week you spent packing one house and moving here, and clearly we wasted three days because of the passport fiasco, but no. You just can't go to work and leave me here. Not today."

I saw the sadness in his eyes as conflicting emotions battled for supremacy. He was longing to get started on the research and his work ethic dictated he should be there. And he knew I needed him, that I believed he had responsibilities at home.

"Look, I'll go in to say hello," he conceded, "and be back by lunch. Honest."

It was the best I was going to get. By nine o'clock, he'd gone.

*

My morning slipped away with feeding Eleanor, then letting her sleep and entertaining Matthew. He sat on my knee on our borrowed chair and we read *The Hungry Caterpillar*. Again. I wrote lists: to do, to buy and to sort out. I unpacked, emptying our clothes into bare wardrobes, shuffling items from one pile to another, hopeful of finding a place to stop. I passed time walking around. Like a baby bird hopping from her nest, I gradually ventured further – out of the door, down the drive, to the main gate of our complex – each step more daring than the first, smothered in sun cream, fearful of the tropical sun. Above all, I waited.

Stephen was back at lunchtime, bursting with news.

"We've been invited out to dinner," he said. "Everyone says hello. They're all really lovely, very friendly and welcoming. I saw Paul up in his office, and he says we can use his driver this afternoon. He's coming in half an hour to take us to Manda Hill."

After a morning of inactivity I found myself rushing around, picking up all the baby paraphernalia required for a shopping trip. Nappies, wipes, bibs, cloths: everything flung together. I collected toy cars and books for Matthew, who complained as I smeared him with more sun cream. I grabbed the lists I had made. I pretended it was possible to tidy up our possessions that were strewn across the bare floors. Passports – remembered them, just in case. Following hours of killing time, I suddenly found myself back in the dilapidated Land Rover – still no car seats – bouncing over to the shops.

The first part of the journey retraced our journey from the airport the previous day. Leaving leafy Kabulonga we cut through Kalingalinga and out to the Great East Road, heading for Manda Hill. Kabulonga was suburbia, one of the wealthier parts of town and filled with embassy houses. It was an easy drive to the American School a few kilometres further out. The houses were all surrounded by high concrete walls, just like ours, topped with barbed wire or broken glass, or ringed by an electric fence. Every gate was large and uncompromising, people shielding themselves from the intense poverty around. I spotted a gardener out on the grass verge scooping water from a plastic oil drum and scattering it over the lawn.

The colour and vibrancy of Kalingalinga was a complete contrast. Gone was sedate wealth. Instead there were people everywhere, walking along the roads, selling their wares, the hustle and bustle of busy working lives. I tried to take in everything I could see

In the shade of the mulberry tree

around me. I was fascinated by the local workmanship, by the industry, by the dust and dirt. I was high up in the Land Rover, looking out over real Africans living and working. I glimpsed their poverty, saw the battered concrete housing that bordered the roadside and the cartoon decoration of a nursery school wall, now faded and chipped by age.

On the other side of the road were piles of rocks, ranging from boulders to gravel. There were trucks from the 1960s tipping sand and cement for the builders, their bonnets proudly proclaiming *British Leyland*. Concrete building blocks were lined up to dry in the sun, with their labourers resting in the shade of a scrawny tree. We passed the local nightclub, the men charging less than a dollar to wash and valet your car, the rows of braai stands and charcoal burners. The place was buzzing with activity, though I had little idea what anyone was doing.

We slowed down as one of the aged trucks ahead of us turned right, slowly creeping across the road, seeming to move the last ten yards solely by driver willpower and the enthusiasm of the men guiding him. I noted a registration plate "EY 16" and wondered how old the vehicle was.

We passed many men in ragged clothes sitting in the dust by the road selling their furniture – pine beds, bookshelves and towel rails from the carpenters; brightly-coloured swings, slides and roundabouts from the metalworkers. There was dust everywhere and the ditch was clogged with rubbish. Furniture was balanced unsteadily at the edge of the trenches, such that I could not be certain whether the perceived asymmetry was due to the positioning or the workmanship. The driver pointed out one of the many carpenters at the roadside.

"That's where Paul got his dining table from."

Our ears pricked up. We had seen the table the previous day and liked its simplicity. "Why did he choose that carpenter?" Stephen asked.

A shrug of the shoulders. "He is good, sir. They are all good, sir," came the unconvincing reply.

Manda Hill was a recently opened shopping centre. It had Shoprite at one side, Game at the other. In between, and down two lengths on the outside, were a variety of shops and banks, mostly South African in origin and many holding no interest at all. I thought I had found a piece of home as I made a beeline to look in Woolworth's; but this was not selling my childhood memories, the sweets by the mini-shovel or the children's toys or music. Disappointingly it was a clothes shop, the last thing I needed right now.

Everywhere there were people: people who seemed to know what they were doing and where they were going. Even though I was battling with our two-seater pram, dodging the sunlight and feeling the heat, I felt safe. The place was not crawling with street vendors or beggars. The shops were selling at fixed prices, clearly labelled. No-one was hassling me, begging me to go into their store: that privilege was left to large window displays and the promise of sale bargains.

The shopping list was long and diverse, but two items took precedence: a mobile phone connection and a fridge. After one long morning at home alone, unsure of when Stephen would be back, I felt a desperate need for the former; the latter's necessity was dictated by the heat and the volume of milk my children drank.

Stephen had decided it didn't matter which network we were on as long as it was the same one, for the call costs were comparable. We headed for the mobile phone outlet he'd used when he first came. The prices were in dollars, with a current rate of exchange into kwacha. Despite a recent change in the law so that everything had to be priced in kwacha, much remained labelled in US dollars, the hard currency of desire. Twenty minutes and a small fortune later, I emerged with a SIM card and a $20 top-up card.

Our next stop, Game, was welcomed for the cool air-conditioning. I could have been at any DIY centre in the UK, looking down its long wide aisles, laden with household goods. We searched out the fridges. Several things were surprising, not least of which was that there was a choice. Having decided on a large fridge and small freezer, with a key to lock it so Matthew could not get in and empty the contents all over our kitchen floor, we were told it could be delivered that day.

"Today?" I asked incredulously. It was already mid-afternoon.

"Yes, Madam."

I looked to Stephen. Firstly, neither of us believed this. Secondly, when would we be back? We decided to play it safe and settled on the next day, in the morning.

A further hour was spent purchasing some food and household basics. A plain, white, plastic picnic table and chairs were bought to function as our dining table, desk and depository for household clobber, as well as a bright yellow table and primary-coloured chairs for the children. Exhausted, we called Paul to ask his driver to come and pick us up. We hadn't thought about how he, his driver, the four of us, a pram, our shopping, two tables and four chairs (of varying sizes) were going to fit in his Land Rover. Clinging once more to my children, this time less for road safety and more to avoid being struck by a loose table leg, we returned home.

Home. Funny how quickly I called it that. Those four walls were my base, the entirety of my present life; the cold brown floors, the blank white walls, the cracked sink and concrete work surfaces. I didn't want to be there, that was true, but I was. I expected to be there for two years. Somehow I had to get through. Somehow I had to survive. Somehow I had to live.

※

True to stereotype, my job was preparing dinner; Stephen's was to put up the new table. It was wobbly. We moved it around the floor to find the most level surface but soon had to acknowledge that it was cheap plastic, not designed to be more than superficially functional. Our planned abuse of it as a desk for computer and studying and a dining table for three meals a day, with Matthew kicking at it in objection to his mother's food, was optimistic.

Still, it was stable enough for dinner and we felt like kings. Eleanor was fed in the pram, the closest thing we had to a high chair. Matthew sat on one plastic chair, boosted by the car seat balanced on top, Stephen on the other, while I sat on the peculiar concrete bench that ran the length of our living room, broken only by the fireplace. Dinner was the local equivalent of Pot Noodles, as a hole remained where the cooker should be. On our shopping trip keeping things cold had taken precedence over making them hot.

※

While Stephen bathed the children I cleared away dinner and pondered what we had. Tanvir, a woman living in another flat on our complex, had left us some old pots and an odd assortment of plates, bowls and mugs. It was her kettle that kept me going with cups of tea. Everything I did seemed to add more purchases to our list: we needed a washing-up bowl and detergent, rubber gloves (could you get Marigolds here?), dishcloths, kitchen roll, dustpan and brush. The children's room needed curtains to encourage them to sleep during the day. A wash-basket would be useful: a week's worth of dirty washing was already piling up on our bedroom floor.

I made mental lists of all the furniture we were missing. Matthew's bed was ordered, but we needed one for ourselves too. The cooker, of course, was a priority. We needed to obtain a sofa and chairs, something that would allow us to sit comfortably. Another table would be useful, so we wouldn't have to clear the laptop and paperwork away before every meal. We needed to organise a telephone line, primarily for the internet. We needed pictures to cover the walls, curtains for privacy, rugs to cover the ghastly brown floor.

In that moment making our house a home became my vocation. I had two choices: live miserly, furnishing with cheap basics for a two-year stint or take this as an opportunity to create a new home for us, free of the inherited furniture back home. I began to dream of the new start I could make.

BLOWING HOT AND COLD

"Are you OK?"

"I'm freezing," I replied, pulling the sheets up around me. The first light of dawn was creeping in through the bedroom window. "I barely slept last night, I was that cold. I thought this was supposed to be Africa!"

Stephen rolled over and gave me a hug. "Better?"

I was reserving judgement. The memory of shivering during the night was still fresh and I was still cold. A quick kiss and Stephen got out of bed.

I asked, "Any chance of a cup of tea, love?"

"Ooh! Cheeky!"

I knew this, but was staying put. There was no way I was setting my feet on that concrete floor any earlier than necessary. On his return he tied up the mosquito net and passed me my tea. "Thank you!" I said, hugging it for warmth. No sooner had I taken a couple of sips than a cry came from next door. I groaned.

"I'll get her," said Stephen, leaping straight back out of bed. Our few moments of early morning peace were gone. Eleanor was brought through for her morning drink; mine had to wait. As I took her I felt how cold her hands were despite having been the most wrapped up of the four of us: pyjamas, a fleecy jumper, a sleeping bag and blankets. I resolved to put another blanket on the next night.

Matthew joined us on the mattress, bringing teddy and a pile of books for his daddy to read to him. Snuggled up on the bed together I felt more like we were a normal family.

It was our third day in Zambia and Stephen returned from work later that morning with the use of Paul's driver for a couple of hours. Our first plan was to sort out bank accounts, so we could get easy access to our money from home. Secondly, we had to buy some sheeting for our beds so that we could return what we had borrowed to Richie. I had added blankets to that list: clearly we needed them too.

The bank was straightforward: Stephen went in and returned with a bundle of forms to complete. Unsurprisingly they required lots of personal identification and forms completed in triplicate, but the tellers seemed very confident about the ease of opening an account, cheerily explaining that if we just brought copies of our passports and birth certificates it would be done within a couple of days.

The bank was close to Kabulonga; the material shops were downtown, in Kabwata. The shops and markets of central Lusaka had certain notoriety – not so much of physical danger, but the high probability of theft and pickpocketing. Every white person was viewed as rich and thus ripe for exploitation. The driver knew exactly where to take us and pulled up outside a shop called Lamisse.

"Are you coming in?" Stephen asked me.

I shook my head. The street was thronging with people, customers were bustling in and out through a narrow doorway. I was convinced every single one would try to steal from my backpack. My unvoiced argument was that I would be safest in the car with Matthew and Eleanor.

"Are you sure?" he said.

"Yes. It's best I stay with the kids. They'll only cause chaos in the shop and I don't want to lose Matthew," I lied.

"OK. So we need a set of sheets and pillowcases for our bed."

"Two, so we can wash them," I corrected, "and a blanket."

"And you trust me with the design?"

I nodded. "Keep it simple."

We'd discussed this earlier: he knew the sort of thing I liked. I wanted something plain, a colour that wouldn't show every dust particle that floated around the house. I waited in the Land Rover, making polite but stilted conversation with the driver. I struggled to concentrate as I was unused to his accent; besides I was constantly on the lookout for thieves in the crowd and anxious for Stephen's return.

Eventually he appeared, carrying his purchases in flimsy carrier bags, which were flung in the back of the vehicle.

"How much were they? How much have we got left?" I asked as he climbed into the passenger seat and slammed the door shut. I was struggling to come to terms with the currency but I knew we didn't have much cash until the bank account was up and running.

In the shade of the mulberry tree

"There's still about half a million kwacha left," Stephen said.

"Enough for a rug?" I hated stepping out of bed onto the cold floor in the morning and I was beginning to think a rug was not a luxury but a necessity.

"Possibly. I need to get some hooks for hanging the mosquito nets securely in the bedrooms, so you can have a look in Game while we're there."

We carried on to the relative comfort of Manda Hill, where I blew half our money on the least offensive rug I could find. The nets remained fixed to the ceiling with drawing pins.

∽

On reaching home I got my first chance to look at the sheets. The packages were pulled out from their bags, displayed in all their glory. Each pack consisted of two sheets and two pillowcases, four packs in total, all identical. Over a foul creamy-brown wavy pattern there were large green leaf shapes and brown stalks the length of the sheet. I was horrified: this was not what I had envisaged. I was looking for something plain and simple, a solid colour that would give some basis for my room design. This was brash and unpleasant.

Still, I told myself, it is a sheet. It cost next to nothing and it would do. No-one needed to see my bedroom except me (well, and Stephen, but he had chosen them): it would serve its purpose. The thin grey flannel blankets would cover up the worst of the design faux pas, even if they provided little in the way of warmth.

How was I going to survive the cold? I wondered. We had been told before we left that June and July were winter and that it was cold, but we'd largely dismissed it. After all, this was tropical Africa, where the sun always shines. Our Ghanaian experience had been of stifling heat building up to sudden, heavy downpours. Even at night, air-conditioning was a necessity. Feeling cold, cold through to the bone, was out of the question. I sighed: it appeared that Zambia was different.

I looked out of the window at the scrappy garden, engulfed in shadows from the mulberry tree. It kept the worst of the sun away from the windows and roof and Richie, trying to help me see the positive side to life here, told me that we would probably be grateful for it by October when it would get really hot. He was right, but in June the cooling effect was unwelcome. The slat windows enabled light and wind to come in and, with the heavy mosquito netting, kept most of the bugs out. But the windows were draughty, particularly where there were panes missing. The heat of the sun was wasted high in the branches of trees and as newcomers to Africa we were shivering from dusk to dawn.

I went through and stripped the bed of the borrowed sheets. Then I discovered that our cheap double bed sheets didn't actually fit our double bed. I could have wept, but it was too late to take them back. As I stood there pondering the insolvable sheet problem – how to get a small sheet to fit a larger mattress – there was a knock at the door.

"Hello!" our neighbour, Tanvir, called out cheerfully. "How are you? How are you settling in?"

"Oh, fine, fine," I smiled in reply. Just don't dwell on the sheets, I was thinking.

"Good, good. This is Precious," she said, introducing the Zambian woman behind her, who was removing her sandals and placing them neatly outside the door. We greeted each other formally, she with a neat little bob and nod of the head, me with the offer of a hand to shake. She was smiling broadly and was dressed in a crimson red T-shirt, with a long piece of brightly-coloured cloth wrapped around her middle like a sarong. I liked her instantly.

"She came and cleaned round before you arrived. I spoke with Stephen earlier and agreed that she might help a little this week – perhaps this afternoon and Friday?"

"That sounds great. I'm not sure what there is to do – some washing? Some cleaning? Is that OK?"

"Yes, that is OK," Precious said with an unwavering smile.

"That sounds fine," agreed Tanvir.

"Oh no, hang on a moment." It dawned on me that it was all very well giving Precious some work but I didn't have any equipment for her. "What do you need to clean with? I just have some dishcloths and washing-up liquid at present."

"Broom?" Precious asked.

I felt guilty. "No – not yet."

"No worries," said Tanvir. "She can use mine for now, just while you get sorted. Precious – can you go back and get the broom and mop?"

"No problem!"

I couldn't quite get over how cheery Precious was. The smile never faltered as she slipped her shoes back on and headed off to the other flat.

"I'm so sorry, Tanvir, you seem to be rescuing me from all my disorganisation."

She laughed. "It isn't an issue. There is no need to return the plates and cutlery at all. The rest can wait a while. You get yourself sorted: I am sure there are more important things to be resolved than a few bits of kitchen cleaning stuff."

Smiling, I thanked her profusely, and then asked the most dangerous question: what do I pay Precious? Tanvir explained what she paid and it seemed very reasonable: no, I was getting a bargain. I was still thinking in terms of the UK and sterling: where could I get a cleaner's services for £1 for an afternoon in London? Crisis gripped me again: was I being fleeced or was I exploiting the worker? I knew wages here were going to be low, I knew I was expected to employ a maid (if not a gardener as well), but I realised I had no idea what the going rate was for domestic staff. Still, for now I trusted Tanvir. Tomorrow I was meeting Natalie, a Belgian woman who was about to leave the country. Amongst other things, she was selling us her water filter and hoping that we would employ her maid when she was gone. I decided I'd ask her what she paid her maid and what she thought the going rate was, then I'd have two opinions to base my decision upon.

Our conversation was interrupted by a commotion at the back door. Stephen was guiding the gardeners in with a cooker borrowed from another flat in the complex. While I knew it was only for a couple of months I was bowled over by this act of generosity.

I said a slightly hurried goodbye to Tanvir and went through to help supervise. I quickly realised I was surplus to requirements, probably just in the way. And even if I did feel useless I was delighted to have a cooker. At last there was the prospect of hot meals: pasta, rice, a baked potato. And a grill would mean toast – toast and marmalade for breakfast, soldiers and a boiled egg for Matthew later.

I leant against the door jamb, watching. Stephen was hands on, supervising the connection to the mains – electric cables left open on the floor, now tied in a slightly less dangerous fashion to the cooker itself, although there was still an exposed length of copper wire. Then the cooker was pushed into position and the dodgy wiring was hidden from sight.

Precious was back and already sweeping up in the living room. I dashed around, tidying things away or, more accurately, out of her way. Astonishingly, great piles of orange dust were collected despite only having been there a couple of days and I was grateful we had arranged for her to come again at the end of the week. She retraced her steps once more to Tanvir's for a floor cloth, cleaning liquid and washing powder, while I returned to writing shopping lists.

∽

As I went to bed that evening I realised that I had never been back to the bedroom to change the sheets. I rushed through to the bathroom and then the living area, but Precious had efficiently washed the borrowed sheets; indeed, an afternoon in the sun had been sufficient for them to dry as well.

"Are you sure we can't risk last night's sheets?" I asked Stephen, more in hope than expectation. At least they had fitted over the mattress.

"No!" He was quite short. "The putzi flies lay their eggs in the damp sheets as they are drying, and then with contact the larvae bury themselves under your skin and grow to become maggots. They-"

"Enough! Enough! I get it! I'll buy an iron and, in the meantime, we'll sleep in these new ones."

He had the grace to look a bit sheepish. "I'm sorry they're not right. I bought the nicest looking design there was. And they are a double size according to the label."

I sighed. "I know. It's OK. We'll make do."

Climbing carefully into bed, so as not to dislodge the sheets such that I ended up on bare mattress, I thought about Precious. She was so happy, quietly getting on with the work. She was completely unfazed that we didn't have a washing machine and seemed quite prepared to wash everything by hand in the bath, including the nappies. I realised, sheets aside, it had been a day full of successes. Bank accounts were in progress, I'd taken my first experiments in the employment of staff, obtained the use of a cooker (and eaten an excellent hot dinner as a result) and I expected to benefit from the bedside rug first thing in the morning. Even the fire we lit burnt well and Stephen was optimistic that the next time it would smoke less. Drifting off to sleep I realised that if we could keep making progress at this rate I could come to quite enjoy myself.

IN NEED OF SHERRY

The next day dawned, as bright and sunny as the previous three. The bottom sheet was rumpled, coming away from the edge by my head, and the top sheet had exposed my toes at the bottom. Stephen lay skedaddled across the whole riotous mess. Last night's optimism had vanished. This did not feel like progress and my mood plummeted once more.

After breakfast I ran round the house tidying up again as I was expecting Natalie and her maid, Sherry. I had to tidy before she arrived as I could not have her thinking we lived in a mess like this all the time, even if we did.

I was terribly anxious about meeting Sherry. She was a complete stranger; somehow even more so than Precious. We had Precious on loan for a few days, but Natalie was hoping that we would want to employ

Sherry when she returned to Belgium. The start of my relationship with her was important since she would become part of our lives for the next two years. Sherry had been a maid in Natalie's family for over fifteen years: she would have everything sorted. I was a novice, new to Africa and new to managing household staff. I feared it would be me being interviewed and assessed rather than her.

Mid-morning they arrived, Natalie doing the introductions. Sherry smiled and bobbed a curtsy, but it was a quieter, less confident beginning than with Precious. She was a large, 'traditionally built' woman, wearing a simple uniform of blue gingham with an apron that helpfully had 'Sherry' embroidered across the front and a green and black jumper, very Eighties in style. I wondered if she would work, if she'd fit in, if she'd be anything like Precious.

We all clambered into the back of Natalie's minibus. She had four children so this was a sensible mode of transport for her family. It too was for sale, but I didn't get the hard sell. Once more I was forced into local child road safety, so held onto Eleanor as Matthew was carefully strapped in. He had strict instructions to sit still, not to fidget, wriggle or undo the seatbelt. He nodded obediently, far too overwhelmed by the situation to do anything other than as he was told.

Natalie drove us into town, pointing out the High Courts, an impressive building overlooking a complicated roundabout. Travelling down Independence Avenue she indicated the Cathedral, various government buildings, the National Museum, the Freedom Statue and then took a turn off to Kabwata. By now I was completely disorientated, but she found a parking space outside the store with a boy to watch over the car. ("Only use him," she said. "You must be careful here.")

In the shade of the mulberry tree

Inside I looked for material to make curtains for the children's room. I wanted something heavy and dark to keep out the daytime light. I shifted Eleanor from one hip to the other, while trying to keep track of Matthew. I could see Sherry talking to him, bending over to ask what he liked; he was shy and not sure what to say to her. After a good look round I decided this shop was not right: the materials were all either light cotton or silky, and few of the patterns were suitable for a nursery. I became more interested in the array of plastic buckets, chairs and tables, thinking that maybe I should start furnishing the house with these in an attempt to tidy away the paraphernalia.

Returning to the vehicle, Natalie took me across the other side of Independence Avenue to Safique's. "This is their new shop," she explained. "I always go here now – the parking is safe and it has all the same materials."

Eleanor was now tetchy and grumpy. I could not reason why: she was well fed and had a reasonable sleep that morning. Wriggling, squirming and whining, she certainly did not seem keen to go inside another shop hunting for material. Matthew resented her getting all the attention and tugged at my skirt, wanting to go.

"Let me take her," said Sherry. I looked at this woman with her gentle smiling face; yet I was scared to give my baby daughter to her. It felt a big step to leave Eleanor with anyone, and Sherry was a complete stranger. Moreover, she was the employee of a complete stranger. I'd barely been here three days and I was entrusting my most treasured possessions to a distant acquaintance.

"She'll be fine with Sherry," chirruped Natalie.

"Are you sure?" I asked Sherry directly.

In need of Sherry

She leant over to take Eleanor, a broad smile stretching across her face as she made eye contact with my little girl. Eleanor stopped wailing immediately.

"Mum!" Matthew tugged again at my skirt.

"You'll come and get me if there are any problems?" I said to Sherry as I clambered down from the minibus.

"No problem, Madam."

I glanced round anxiously as I took my little boy's hand and headed inside the shop.

On entering, my concerns about Eleanor were pushed to the back of my mind. It was a veritable Aladdin's cave of cloth, hanging from the rafters, roll after roll stacked along the walls. I gazed in amazement at the double height room, surprisingly light and airy. All around were African cloths – chitenge, waxed and unwaxed, their bright colours decorating the room. There was netting and lining material, soft cottons and silky satins, heavy upholstery materials and pin-striped suiting. I found some thick cotton with elephants on and decided this would do: it seemed more robust than the thin yellow material with orange teddy bears and more childlike than a simple striped pattern.

Purchases made, we returned to the car. Sherry didn't appear to have moved, but Eleanor had found peace and satisfaction, fast asleep in her arms. I climbed in beside them, quietly, trying not to disturb my beautiful baby daughter. Both she and Sherry had utterly contented smiles upon their faces. With that, the decision was made: Sherry had the job.

Natalie started up the engine and we returned home. Precious only worked part-time for Tanvir, so why not employ her as well? Full-time childcare and daily cleaning I claimed as a personal treat to compensate for being in this foreign land.

BESPOKE FURNITURE

Nearing the end of our first week it was clear that our plastic table was never going to be sufficiently robust for our abuse. It had a prodigious dip in the middle which made it difficult to write on. The previous day Stephen sat at it with his laptop and found the table slid away from him across the floor. We wedged it into the corner so it could not move any further. This solved one problem, but Stephen still needed a good desk for working at home; and so we decided to try the carpenter in Kalingalinga that Paul's driver had recommended.

We had never had anything custom-made before. After the children had gone to sleep we got the measuring tape and creatively designed our dining table. Laying the blanket from our bed on the floor gave an idea of the table size; the garden chairs were there to

Bespoke furniture

ensure that others would fit round with room to manoeuvre. We quickly discovered that the room appeared large because it had nothing in it.

"How much space do we need? I mean, there are four of us. Is a square enough?"

"I'm hoping we'll have some friends to visit," I said. "Wouldn't it be better if we can get, for example, your parents at the table with us as well?"

"Hmm…yes. Six people will require…" With this Stephen measured out using the chairs to get a comfortable length. "There!" He stood back, proud of his layout. "Will six be enough? What if a family come for dinner?"

"Or perhaps birthday parties? Can we squeeze eight chairs in?"

We crawled around on the floor, rearranging the blanket to different table sizes. We laid it lengthways and across the room. We placed the chairs at either end, estimating the amount of legroom required to stand up from the table. Recalling an article I'd read, I fetched a magazine from the bedroom and read up on the different sizes of dining chairs. A feat of complicated mathematics and a vast amount of guesswork decided the final dimensions.

We took the measurements to the carpenter. Kelvin worked behind a run-down nursery school, his basic furniture displayed at the roadside. There was a group of men wandering around his wares, some idly chatting; others keen to entice any would-be purchaser. Around the back was his workshop, a lean-to of battered roofing and ground covered with sawdust. Some young men were sanding and planing wood at the far end, a few looked busy and others were actually working. Kelvin was of indeterminable age, his weathered face hidden behind a wild beard, possibly the result of tropical sun, manual work or the strains of living on the poverty line. He stooped over his workbench, looking in detail at our sketch and measurements, but he was surprisingly tall when he straightened up to talk.

"What type of wood?"

"Like Mr Paul," Stephen replied.

"How do you want the legs? Straight? With a bar?"

"How did Mr Paul have it?"

"Tapered, like this," he said, drawing a quick sketch on a scrap of paper.

"Yes, like Mr Paul," Stephen replied.

"Waxed or varnished?" he asked.

"What was Mr Paul's?"

"Waxed."

"Waxed it is then."

In this manner our first ever item of bespoke furniture was designed and ordered.

※

A couple of days later we were back. It had struck us that, given we were paying about £200 for this table and chairs we could design it however we wanted, rather than the standard size and shape. Being a great fan of Charles Rennie Mackintosh I had seen a picture of some elegant chairs and suddenly thought: why don't I get them like that?

Trying to explain turn-of-the-century Scottish architect-styled furniture to a simple Zambian carpenter was easier said than done. From our perspective only one change was required: the seat backs needed to be elongated. Ideally I would have added in a carved rose or some geometric squares that were also the signature of Mackintosh's style. But it was the disproportionately tall backs that would clinch it.

Yet, from Kelvin's perspective, the wood had already been bought and some of the legs had already been turned. He brought one to show us: a beautiful piece of woodturning indeed. I hesitated, uncertain what to say or do. They were not really in line with the simple, straight, square design I liked.

The customer is always right: that is the joy of custom-made furniture. True to the British stereotype I didn't want to upset him or cause a scene. A little negotiation over the price, a small delay in their preparation, and our designer dining table and chairs were back on track.

"Next week," he said confidently.

I couldn't wait.

RESORTING TO CHOCOLATE

Week two, and my first full day without Stephen. After my protestations the previous Monday he tried hard to just work mornings. Now he said he really had to go to the hospital full-time, for it was the work that paid for us to be there. Then his clinching argument came.

"Besides, the sooner I get the research done, the quicker we can go home."

᭥

I wandered around my bare house wondering what to do. There was so much to be done, given we were missing many of life's basic comforts, such as furniture and curtains. We remained sleeping on mattresses on the floor. Kelvin may have promised us the table and chairs within a week, but in the meantime we just had one wooden chair borrowed from Richie, its thin cushions being the only comfort for me when breastfeeding. Natalie's daughter was kindly sewing the curtains for the children's room, but I still had to find a seamstress to make the rest. Nor did I yet have the courage to go shopping for more material.

Despite the ever-lengthening list of things to do, I couldn't motivate myself to start any of them: partly from not knowing where to begin, partly as we were without transport, but mainly overwhelming fear. I was afraid of being fleeced by the taxi drivers or taken for a ride by the market traders. I was worried that items in the house might go missing: I'd been warned to be careful about leaving anything valuable out in front of staff. Not that there was much of any value, but every day the laptop had to be hidden safely away at the back of the wardrobe, our limited cash secreted in different hidey-holes.

Briefly I wondered about calling home, but we had no landline connected to the house. Allegedly the man from Zamtel was coming the following day, but then again, that is what they had claimed all week. No telephone line also meant no internet connection. I was taken aback by how dependent I was upon these in London, but now…did it really matter? The mobiles were prohibitively expensive to both call from and to, so I had heard nothing from my family, although Stephen sent a brief message from an internet café the day after we landed to say that we had arrived safely. It was like being marooned on an island: I had enough to survive, but the lack of communication with the rest of the world weighed heavily upon me.

Precious came through from the bedroom.

"Excuse me," she said, "there's a mosquito in Eleanor's cot."

My heart missed a beat.

"Let me see!" I cried out, as I rushed through to the children's room. Precious followed.

"There," she said, pointing to the blanket.

And he was – the nasty blighter out to kill my daughter. Precious and I looked at him for a few moments. I wasn't sure what to do. He was larger than I expected, maybe a centimetre long, with a solid body, thin, distinct head, thorax and abdomen, long arched legs. It struck me that memorising what he looked like would be of benefit, should any others dare to appear. Stephen said there weren't mosquitoes in Lusaka in the dry season, but here was one: I could see him gently moving, breathing but, if I was honest, not actually doing anything. What was I supposed to do?

I looked up at Precious. She was still staring at the mosquito. I looked back down. No change.

"Can we kill him?" I asked.

Precious shrugged her shoulders. "Yes," but this was more of an 'I s'pose so' than the cravings of an out-and-out mosquito murderer. Still, she reached into the cot and squashed him, before returning to her tasks.

One down, how many to go?

Not for the first time, I wondered why Stephen wasn't there when I needed him. When my children both had heavy, feverish colds a few months earlier he was in Switzerland at a conference. I spent the nights running up and down the stairs panicking about their poor health; he slept soundly in a hotel room. What benefit did I get from being married to a paediatrician with a diploma in tropical medicine if he wasn't around when I actually found a tropical disease carrier in my daughter's cot? It was his choice to come to Zambia, but I was the one facing the diseases.

I was angry, fearful and lonely all at once. Why were we in this dreadful place? I didn't want to be here, not one jot.

I calmed myself down with some chocolate left over from our flight the previous week. Matthew toddled up and I succumbed to his big brown eyes.

"Here you are," I said, giving him a bit. Together we bit in, savouring the taste as it slipped down our throats – although in Matthew's case there was a fair proportion spreading across his face, T-shirt and hands.

"Let's walk down to the shops," I said as I cleaned him up and gave his T-shirt a cursory wipe. His protestations made me refrain from wetting the whole thing and I decided we'd venture into the outside world just as we were: chocolate and all.

※

There were two Melissa supermarkets in Lusaka. The one in Kabulonga was a little bit more expensive than the one at Northmead, so I was told, but that is what I paid for living in the posh part of town. The cheapest food was in the city centre: in no way was I ready to venture there yet. The other supermarkets varied, and the only way to find a good deal was to go round them all and pick the best offer in each. It was a laborious exercise. In Zambia everything varied (produce and price) from week to week, from day to day, even from morning to afternoon.

Reaching our destination, I relished the cool air of the store after the heat of the ten-minute walk. As with so many buildings in Africa, it had been designed to keep cool, rather than having to rely on air-conditioning. I started with an investigation of the fruit and vegetables. Most was unappetising. I didn't know what to do with gem squash nor would we ever get through such large bags of chillies. I didn't know what all the strange leaves were – cassava, rape, pumpkin leaves... I pounced upon the broccoli. There was none of this the previous week. Also I saw some packaged mangetout and sugar snaps.

I battled again with the exchange rate: dividing by 7500 had never been my strong point. The broccoli was pricey; however, it didn't take much to realise the K900 for the mangetout was virtually nothing. There was quite a mark-up from producing country to Western fridge.

I walked on, picking up some milk and a five-litre bottle of water. Matthew would have to walk back as I could not carry them and push the pram. They took his seat in the pushchair while he investigated the boxes along the floor at the bottom of the fridges.

The meat counter was ahead, which I dutifully looked at. Being vegetarian I was uncertain which meat was appropriate for different recipes, but I did know that flies and a greyish-green tinge were not a good start. I was obliged to buy some for Sherry and Precious to eat. I had been told it was a traditional perk of the job that the maid has food provided by the employer, and that beef was cheap. I got the reddest chunks I could and hoped they were satisfactory.

Next, baby food. There was a limited range of jars, mainly for babies younger than mine. I picked up a familiar trio: apple, carrot and mixed vegetables. I longed for the arrival of our shipment containing the handheld liquidiser so I could make some fresh and healthy mushy food for Eleanor. I reluctantly picked up some powdered milk. For years we had sworn off buying Nestlé goods in protest at their promotion of milk powder rather than breastfeeding. What irony then, that I should be in Zambia and forced to purchase the one thing I objected to in order that my daughter would sleep with a satisfied stomach.

Some cereal, some pasta and we were done.

Resorting to chocolate

At the till Matthew was transfixed by some low-shelved sweets. I was forced to smile at his innocence and really didn't have the energy to argue or tell him off.

"Oh, all right!"

I bought something to sustain him on his walk home – or perhaps just to sustain me, as a grumpy toddler is never any fun, particularly when feeling fragile myself.

The walk back was slow. Matthew toddled along, finding a remarkably large number of things to distract him. But I was grateful for the ambling pace: what had I to look forward to? The concrete mausoleum. Bare walls and an echo, like it was constantly calling for someone it had lost. I longed for curtains to brighten up the rooms, paintings on the walls and a large, squishy sofa I could collapse into at the end of the day.

Getting home, Matthew ran through to the bedroom, waking his sister in the process. Sherry was there for him: soon I could hear them making revving engine noises together. I tuned the kitchen radio to the BBC World Service, thinking this might cheer me up, while I put away the shopping. I had hoped it would keep me up-to-date with British news but all I heard about was American elections and the invasion of Iraq. Ten minutes of news and nothing from the UK. So much for the *British* Broadcasting Corporation.

I switched it off, took a glass of water from the fridge and looked round. Sherry had cleaned and tidied: I didn't even have the menial tasks to do. I crumpled into one of our plastic garden chairs and held my head in my hands. All I was doing was marking time until we returned home – home for a holiday, better still, home for good.

MOTHERING IN ZAMBIA

Tuesday morning and I was pushing the pram around the corner to a playgroup that I had been told about. It was only our second week in the country but I needed to find someone else to talk to and my children were the best way in. The weekly round of mums and toddlers groups in London had saved Matthew and me from mutual boredom.

The directions were to go to the end of our road, turn left and then take the first gate on the left. It all seemed simple enough, although when I reached the blue gate there was no indication that a playgroup was inside.

I tapped tentatively on the metal gate. No response.

Taking a step back, I looked up and down the road to make sure I hadn't missed anything, but this was the first gate and there were no signs that I should be anywhere else.

I tapped again, more confidently this time, but the watchman still didn't open up.

I was about to admit defeat when a large four-wheel drive pulled in (we had to move out of the way quite sharply) and blasted its horn loudly three times. Like 'open sesame', the gate swung wide to let the vehicle through. I crept in behind it, just squeezing past before the guard slammed the doors shut. I asked hesitantly if I was in the right place. He looked me up and down, as if I was a creature from another planet, and then nodded.

"Yes, Madam," and pointed in the direction the car had gone.

The playgroup was run by a woman called Rachel. She was a bit surprised by our arrival but graciously welcomed us in. Her garden was set out as a pre-schooler's paradise. There were swings and slides, a Wendy house, a table with playdough, another with colouring and sticking equipment and rugs laden with toys: Lego, cars and dolls. I stayed to see my children settled, although I had no reason to be concerned. Matthew was in his element, loving the games, the other children and the vast array of 'new' toys. Eleanor charmed the maids and played contentedly on the rug with them.

I was in awe of the way Rachel encouraged all the children and kept them interested in their activities. They all stopped for juice and a biscuit and then she read them a couple of stories. Matthew was entranced. I recognised being in the presence of genius.

"Can we come next week?" I asked Rachel at the end. I was struggling to extract Matthew from the painting equipment and could see this session as a lifeline for me: a couple of hours to myself every week.

In the shade of the mulberry tree

"That will be fine," she replied.

What I now needed to do was find other activities that would entertain a toddler. Perhaps I could persuade Stephen to take us for lunch at a restaurant I'd heard of that had a children's play area?

As I was strapping Eleanor back into the pram I overheard another mother talking to Rachel.

"Thank you so much for today," she said. "Can I bring my friend next time? She has two boys."

Rachel hesitated. "I'm sorry, but really I'm full."

I heard the discomfort in her voice, perhaps even knowing that I was within earshot. Matthew and Eleanor had been allowed to stay and I realised that I was exceptionally lucky. I left quickly before she changed her mind.

∽

"Turn right at the crossroads – yes, I guess that's here – then straight on at the next…yes, she said it became a dirt road…" I was relaying instructions to our taxi driver who had hit the dusty orange dirt road with speed, and I winced as he bounced and scraped along. He dodged the worst of the ruts and rocks and used the grassy kerbside to keep level. We passed between the two big trees and I told him to take the next road on the left and look out for the numbered gate. I clutched Eleanor tightly with one arm and used the other to hold Matthew back. For a two-and-a-half-year-old he was sitting very calmly on the back seat, but the uneven road and uncertainty about where we were going were causing his mother to be on edge.

We arrived just behind a white Land Cruiser. Anxious to know if I was in the right place, I was relieved to see Kelly emerge. We had met, quite by chance, in a café at the weekend, her son being a shade younger than Eleanor. While talking she had mentioned a group of mums and toddlers who met every Wednesday and had written down instructions.

She gave me a wave of recognition, coming over as I got out of the taxi.

"You found the place OK?"

"Yes – your directions were perfect."

"Very Zambian in style – no road names, just 'turn left after the trees'. Amazingly, it works!"

I laughed in agreement. She introduced me to our hostess and together we walked with her round to the back of the house.

My anxiety about the directions for getting here was only exceeded by my anxiety about meeting the other mothers. Once more, I was creating a first impression. I needed to make friends and I find small talk such an exhausting experience. Some people are naturally gifted at it, and I rely on them being the people I meet. When I come across another naturally shy and self-conscious person, conversation is stilted, staccato and full of silences. Long, awkward silences.

The mothers were a mixed bunch of different nationalities and I was struck by the colourful children: white, black, brown; blonde, dark and ginger. This was truly a chocolate box assortment. They all played riotously together, though at first Matthew needed a bit of encouragement to join in. Eleanor sat on a rug and smiled with the other babies. Having lost his inhibitions Matthew was keen to follow one boy into the largest paddling pool I had ever seen: it was a small swimming pool. The other boy had to wear armbands and I had to hold Matthew back. I made a mental note to bring swimming costumes next time.

Although pleasant, I was relieved when the afternoon was over. I was overwhelmed by the mothers I met. They all seemed so settled, so confident, so assured of whom and where they were. I was not. Or rather, I was quite sure I was not meant to be there. Even that I questioned: clearly I was meant to be there, as I followed my husband and his work, but it was only for my love of him that I landed in this particular place.

My head ached from the accumulation of social knowledge. Everything was so new, so incomprehensible. I needed a new mindset to cope with the cultural and practical differences. I felt drained by being on best behaviour all the time, from smiling at everything and everyone. It all seemed an act, but a part I had to endure if I was to get any enjoyment out of the two years at all.

❦

The three weeks we had been given as 'Visitors' by Immigration had almost passed and we were anxious to get permission to stay. They required evidence of Stephen's qualifications before they would release his work permit, and then one stamp in our passports would enable us to live in Zambia for two years. That was all we required: by then Stephen's work would be complete and we could all return to London. "The sooner I get the research done, the quicker we can go home," as Stephen had said.

Our brush with the bank had introduced us to Zambian bureaucracy: everything had to be signed and stamped and authorised. The Head of Medicine was to be available at 14.30: our responsibility was to be there with copies of our certificates – professional, birth, passports – so he could sign to say they were true copies of the originals. We were on time; we waited for him to be ready.

It was my first visit to UTH, the University Teaching Hospital. It was a vast building, sprawling over a mile down Nationalist Road. Our taxi brought us in past the paediatric buildings at the top of the hill, proudly declaring their recent funding from an international pharmaceutical company. We wound our way down past nurses' buildings and the maternity section, before coming in a back route to the main blocks. Stephen already seemed totally orientated, pointing out where Paul worked, where the High-cost Care rooms were and the location of each department. At the far end was the virology lab, where Stephen would be most of the time, doing research with the samples taken from his patients at the other end of the complex. I began to understand why he had talked about getting a bicycle: it was a long way from the lab to the ward and back again.

Our certificates were duly signed and stamped. We showed effusive gratitude and then walked up to paediatrics, Stephen continuing his guided tour en route.

The malnutrition ward was towards the back, a small, single-storey concrete building with open windows. Inside there were heaters, keeping warm the small bags of bones that ought to be children. The electric bars burned the dust, a smell curiously mixed with the sharp hygiene of bleach, but overall was the pervading scent of sickness.

Everywhere I turned there was a sick child. The room was packed with beds: high-sided metal cots with two babies per mattress. They all lay immobile, deathly quiet, some hooked up to a drip. Their eyes were wide open, staring at nothing, although noticing me – the bright white face – as I peeked over to say hello. Other than the bulging eyes there was no response, children too weak to move, or even smile.

Beside the cots were mothers, sitting, waiting for an improvement. They were also thin and immobile, trapped by their patience and maternal hope for a miraculous return to health. The odds were against them. A couple of women cupped their hands and bowed to me. It was a sign of respect to the white woman, but why? It was only my skin colour. I could do nothing to help, having no medical knowledge to speak of. I caught one mother's tear-laden eyes and smiled encouragingly. But what use was that to her? I am no different to you, I thought. If it were one of my children lying in that hospital bed, I would also be heartbroken, unable to move, clinging to hope for survival.

A fly shot past my nose. A 'bzzt' and the blue light had taken it.

The nurses moved about silently, the occasional cheery comment to encourage, but mainly remaining at the nursing station fiddling about with paperwork. Stephen met and greeted a few people that he knew. I waited at a distance, nodding and smiling to the nurses. How hopeless and helpless I was. Just twenty-four hours earlier I was with a group of mothers, laughing and joking, drinking tea and eating biscuits. Here, laid out before me, were people without enough money to buy even the cheapest nshima to eat.

"I've just got to see one more patient and then we can go," Stephen said.

"OK." I smiled weakly. He was still talking, describing the girl he was concerned about. She was nothing but bones and skin. I was barely listening.

For the first time I truly understood why Stephen felt the need to leave our comfortable London lifestyle to work in Africa. I had seen pictures like these on television, read articles in the newspapers, been inundated with appeals from charities. I had been moved by such images, concerned about their welfare, but it was no substitute for being here. I was in the middle of the situation, looking starvation and poverty in the face.

BLANKET BARGAINING AND BUYING

Beginning to understand why Stephen was working here did not eradicate my own problems. The nights were getting colder and I was growing more miserable. Eleanor's sleeping habits, at nine months old, still depended upon very early mornings, which didn't sit naturally with me. Matthew woke with nightmares at least twice a week and my night-time wanders to comfort him necessitated bare feet on the concrete floor, cold creeping up my legs. Eventually I would return to bed, but both it and I had cooled down so much that I struggled to get warm.

"Are you OK?"

I pulled the blankets up around my neck. "What do you think?"

Blanket bargaining and buying

Stephen cuddled me, but spooning only warmed half the body. I had shivered for much of the night and I was fed up with it.

"It will get warmer," he said.

It couldn't get colder. Uncharitable thoughts flooded my mind. I hated beginning the day this way: I started grumpy and, exhausted from lack of sleep, got moodier as time progressed. "We need more blankets."

I might have been stating the obvious but our cash flow was running low and we couldn't afford the ones off-the-shelf in Game. I knew: I'd looked. Despite all the bank's assurances, opening an account was not straightforward and took several weeks. Now we were waiting for the transfer of funds from the UK and even that had been fraught with difficulty. Meanwhile, we had changed the last of our dollars and were on an economy drive.

"You'll have to go to the market."

I sat up straight and turned to look at Stephen in astonishment.

"Me?"

"Yes. I'm at work all day so you're the one with the time. You can leave the children here with Sherry and take a taxi in."

For some reason, Stephen hadn't fully understood my fear of venturing into the central markets. I was scared stiff of the thronging people and lack of personal space. I was fearful of the bustle, the petty theft and, most of all, the masses of locals versus me, the solitary white woman. I was still very white: I'd barely let my body see the sun.

"But– "

"Don't worry – you'll be fine." There was a hesitation, and I saw he had picked up on my fears. "Why don't you go with Precious? She can help you with the bargaining and show you the way."

I sagged a little. I liked Precious a lot. She was clearly a bright woman and would have a good knowledge of the market and where to go. Surely, having lived her entire life here, she would be adept at bartering with the stallholders and would recognise a good price. It looked like I had no choice.

And so arrangements were made. Precious was deputed to accompany me to the market, supporting the stray, ignorant white woman while Matthew and Eleanor were left with Sherry.

Stephen went in late to work. He put all our money in a bum bag; the empty rucksack in which to carry the blankets back was put on the front of the body, constantly in my line of vision. He bustled around me, ensuring everything was secure, safe, hidden and passed on bits of instruction thinly disguised as advice. "Don't let anyone see where the money is. Keep your eyes open, keep looking around." There were also words of encouragement and support. "Don't worry, Precious will help you."

I was terrified.

We chose not to venture into Soweto Market, the main, sprawling market in the centre of town, but to go to the smaller market situated behind the smart COMESA buildings on Ben Bella Road. The taxi dropped us off outside a row of stalls, piled high with bottles of whisky, vodka and gin. In an aside, Precious told me that most of the bottles were watered down, had fake labels or fell off the back of a truck. I think her term was 'they are not real', but I understood exactly what she meant.

We made our way towards the main body of the market, stepping over the uneven dusty-orange ground and avoiding the rubbish that blew all over, collecting like snowdrifts against the surrounding walls.

The main area had narrow alleys between the permanent stalls, some even with concrete bases. Cheap awnings were rigged overhead, using stripy tarpaulin that had worn through from the tropical sun and flapped dangerously in the breeze. Men came out to greet me, clearly seeing a good candidate for a profitable sale, encouraging me again and again to take a look. I silently screamed for peace and personal space.

"Madam, come – see!"
Stop pestering me! Go away!
"Madam, please, come and look!"
Leave me alone!
"Madam, here, Madam. Beautiful carving!"
I'm not interested!

Petrified, I smiled, glanced quickly and looked down or away, hoping that the fleeting moment of eye contact was no encouragement to them. Then it struck me I might look snobbish, even imperialistic, thinking myself above it all and peering down my nose at the local efforts to make a sale. I snuck a peek at as many wares as possible without looking any of the salesmen in the face.

Dust and rubbish pervaded the walkways, but the stalls were a revelation. None bigger than about two or three metres-squared, they were crammed with as much produce as possible. Clothes were hung from the poles that supported the tarpaulin, rough tables displayed carvings or rolls of material or weaving. There were old women, crouching over a small fire, roasting cobs of corn and young men walking round with bags of groundnuts in baskets on their heads. A heady mix of sweat, charcoal cooking and dust filled the air.

Blankets, it turned out, were not the most popular item for sale. I rushed past the first stall I saw, fearful of being drawn into something I could not control. Besides, the patterns were large, floral designs in amazing lurid colour schemes. Given a secondary aim was to hide our horrendous sheets I was trapped in an agonisingly ugly world. Yet we struggled to find any other stalls selling blankets, which surprised me given it was the middle of their winter. Eventually we found one more selling the same thin grey blankets we already had, and right in the far corner another displayed mock-tartan ones that were marginally thicker. I had to take these hideous blankets seriously as there was no alternative. I looked through the pile to see if there were any I could tolerate gracing my bedroom.

I stepped to one side with Precious to discuss tactics. Precious, I was sure, would be happy with any of these blankets and was probably amazed that I could be so fussy. But I needed some style, something that I could look at and not feel that I was in deepest, darkest Africa. It needed to give me some semblance of home, of the Western world. I also needed to be warm.

The mock-tartan was the best compromise: relatively thick, warm and not too horrific to look at. Returning to that stall we discovered that they didn't have anything more than the one colour scheme that I liked in a double. I had to take it, though I would have been more at ease with a queen-size. I had learnt my lesson with the Lamisse sheets and decided I could always cope with it being too big, but too small just could not be endured. I crouched down and leafed through the basket, eventually choosing a bright red and yellow check that I decided was just about suitable for a toddler boy's bedroom.

The prices were not extortionate, so only light haggling followed before I made my purchases. It was a good start but in order to be warm I needed other blankets too. I wondered at the complexity of procuring something that would be so simple to purchase in a department store back home.

Finally we returned to the first stall we had seen. There I let Precious – the local, used to this type of sale and market – negotiate over the price. The conversation went something like this:

"How much for the blanket?"
"Which one?"
"This one – queen-size."
"160,000 kwacha."
"How about K150,000?"
"K155,000?"
"Oh, that's not good."
"It's my best offer."
"OK then – we'll take two."

Three hundred and ten thousand kwacha later I had two more depressing blankets stuffed into the rucksack and we were escaping the market and the enthusiastic salesmen. In the taxi home I assessed the finances of the trip. I had saved little more than a pound by Precious's mediocre bargaining skills. As a result I paid only a fraction less than I would at the international stores in Manda Hill and had much less aesthetically pleasing blankets. Add in the taxi fares and we were probably break-even.

But at the end of the day, I didn't care. I might not have a great bargain and the stallholders might have exploited my inexperience, but I anticipated snuggling down for the night in a warm, cosy bed with unbroken sleep for the first time in weeks. Bliss.

✧

The last Saturday of the month heralded the craft market at the Dutch Reformed Church. We donned our sunhats and smothered ourselves in sun cream for the walk down the road, but on turning the corner we were taken aback. The usually quiet Kabulonga street had transformed into a four-wheel drive parking lot. Scattered along the road were gentlemen in red tabards, leaping out in front of the traffic, waving the cars into empty spaces. We passed plenty of unofficial attendants as well, all eager for the business of an unsuspecting visitor.

Walking to the market avoided the stress of parking, but still we were bombarded by street hawkers. There was a gentleman who thought we would be delighted to buy a wooden pounder and bowl, and many women with clay pots. Nearer the entrance gate there were woven baskets, floor mops and chickens. We practised our polite refusals the length of the road. "Not today, thank you." There was a sparkle in my eye as I repeated this mantra. Privately I knew I meant, 'Not tomorrow either, if you don't mind.'

Inside, in the cool shade of the trees, sat men with an array of plants or vegetables, women with crocheted blankets, more people with carvings and 'genuine antiques'. At the back of the church we bought tea, coffee or bottled drinks. There were two aisles full of stalls selling food. The aroma of meat on the braai filled the air, but our greatest delight was a diminutive Indian woman who sold Bombay mix. The smallest bag was enough to feed an army, but what a treat!

Under the covered area were clothes, cheap children's toys, second-hand books, soaps and candles. Back outside we wandered past an array of paintings: canvasses pegged to twine strung between the trees. There was some sturdy weaving and basketwork, creating sofas and chairs, tables and bookshelves. There was ironwork, beautifully twisted into candleholders and light fittings.

Everywhere there were people. Locals encouraging us to look at their stalls, wanting us to purchase their postcards or jewellery. Expats enjoyed the sunshine, out for a bargain, buying gifts before their journeys back to a summer in the northern hemisphere. The place was bustling with excitement and life. I didn't find it as threatening or cramped as the COMESA market. Instead it was captivating, a microcosm of Lusakan life.

Nevertheless, I was here on a mission: artwork. Our house's bare, white walls stared back at me every day of the week and the echoes accentuated my loneliness, a hollow sound so empty and abandoned. I had decided that wall hangings would kill two birds with one stone: reduce the noise and cheer up the rooms.

What I hadn't anticipated was to be so unimpressed by the local work. Much of it was repetitious. Black elephant, red-orange sun. Three giraffes, various sizes. Or maybe, if you were lucky, a tree. There were variations on a theme, but choice was limited and clearly mass-produced for the tourist trail.

We walked back and forth along the line. This only excited the salesmen more and I longed to go and hide. One gentleman's collection had a bit of spark, something unusual in his choice of colours and more muted use of gold paint to outline key features. Stephen and I spent some time deciding, changing our minds, returning, negotiating. But the children were crotchety and the pram didn't really like the rocky terrain. Nor did the stallholders, as the wheels ran close to the carvings laid out on the ground.

"I'll take them home," Stephen decided. "You've been at home with these two all week so I'll give you a moment's peace."

I do love him. It was my treat to stay in this buzzing, lively place.

After parting with them at the gate I realised this gift was a double-edged sword. I was left on my own to do the final negotiations on our chosen pictures. Given the failures at the COMESA market I was not filled with confidence.

On getting back to our chosen artist I faced an unexpected problem: the picture that Stephen and I had jointly decided upon had gone. I spent another five minutes trying to decide what the best alternative was. A lot of the colours were unpleasant or gloomy, and the last thing I needed was a picture that brought down my mood.

Eventually I decided upon a cheery yellow square depicting four African musicians as stylised black silhouettes, together with another picture of a typical African woman carrying her baby on her back. The negotiation was straightforward, which left me worrying that I was not as pushy as I should have been. Still, I haggled sufficiently well to save more than Precious did on two expensive blankets earlier in the week.

Carefully carrying my pictures home, I met up with Rachel, laden with a couple of plants and a bag of avocados.

"I'm always worried about being ripped off," I confessed, having explained why I had bought the wall hangings.

"How much did you pay for those?" she asked.

Hoping for some affirmation of my brilliance, I told her.

"That seems all right," she said.

It wasn't the most convincing response. I took solace that I had not been completely fleeced, and it was probably the best answer I could expect in the circumstances. So far that month Rachel – a complete stranger – had saved both my sanity, by looking after my children, and my pride. 'That seems all right,' was what I needed to hear – something that confirmed that I wasn't messing up, that perhaps I would be able to survive in Zambia after all.

TABLE TALK

Bath time was proving to be a riot and, despite all my cajoling, Matthew obstinately refused to put on his pyjamas. Stephen arrived back from work, later than expected, just as Matthew grabbed the offending items of clothing and made a dash for freedom down the corridor.

"Whoa! What's going on here?"

"Hello Daddy!" Matthew skidded to a stop, then landed on his bottom with a giggle. Stephen bent down to help him up. Matthew was all sweetness and light, giving him a huge hug, as if he hadn't seen his father for a week.

"Why are you still up?" he asked. "And, I might add, naked?"

In the shade of the mulberry tree

"A good question," I called from the bathroom. Help had arrived and I was taking a couple of moments to mop up the water and tidy the plastic toys that covered the floor. I could just make out Matthew's innocent answer that he was just going to bed, and Stephen responding that he needed his pyjamas on then. A couple of moments later they appeared in the corridor: one young boy smartly dressed for bed.

"How do you do it?" I asked in amazement. "I've been battling for the last twenty minutes to get him into those clothes! You are officially on bath and bedtime duty from now on."

"Can I have a story, Daddy?"

As I headed for the kitchen I gave Stephen a kiss in passing. "He's all yours!"

∽

It had been several weeks since our arrival but at last I had enough confidence in my equipment and shopping powers to invite Richie over for dinner. We still didn't have a set of crockery with more than three matching plates nor enough cutlery to survive two courses, but I had concocted a simple, one-pot pasta dish. More important than the dinnerware was the mukwa dinner table, which had finally arrived from Kelvin. The hardwood part of mukwa is a dark, warm brown, but is easily streaked with a pale wood, closer to a pine colour. This is softwood and thus susceptible to termites and other borers. Kelvin had worked hard for us to make the table from the dark wood and there were just a few white streaks adding character to the tabletop. I was ridiculously proud of it.

I heard footsteps go past the dining room window and an "oooh!" then a knock on the front door. Richie had arrived.

Table talk

Letting himself in he immediately commented on my pride and joy. "I see the table has arrived. Today?" He pulled out a chair to have a closer look at the carpentry.

"Yesterday. When ordering it we never thought about how to squeeze it through all the doors and round the angles into this room. Thank goodness it is only an archway into the living room and we've no other furniture to block the route. The gardener helped, but he was really struggling to work out how to get it in. Next table: only 73 centimetres tall."

He laughed, whether at our ineptitude or the image of the gardener struggling to get the furniture in was unclear.

"I like the tall chairs," he said. "Very stylish. Worth the extra expense."

I beamed with pride. The Charles Rennie Mackintosh style chair backs had come out exactly as I had wanted. Then Richie's face fell into a frown. "I'm not so sure about the legs," he commented.

"Ah."

"A bit of a mismatch?"

"Yes. Well, we hadn't wanted to hurt Kelvin's feelings so we kept what he had already done."

It was called compromise. Kelvin's elegantly turned front legs were kept, but he purchased more wood (at our expense) to make the straight backs. 'Compromise' involved us paying more money for just part of what we wanted. I suspected that we were not grown up enough yet to have bespoke furniture made for us.

I hid my embarrassment by offering Richie a drink.

"Thanks. How are you settling in?" Richie asked as I reached for a coke.

"Hmm…" I paused to weigh up the right answer. "Fine."

"Fine?"

"Fine," I asserted. I was not committing to more, and my resolution was to make the best of the way the die had rolled, to remain as positive as I could about the African experience. "Bits and pieces are falling into place. It all seems to take such a long time to organise. I'm in a constant battle with Zamtel to get a telephone line put in, the bank requires yet more documentation in order to put money into our account and the other day I had ZESCO at the door threatening to cut off our electricity for non-payment."

"And you've paid?"

"It is an issue with a previous tenant, not us, but it was a scary moment."

Richie let his breath out. "My approach, for what it's worth, is to achieve one thing each day. It doesn't matter what it is, but then anything else is a bonus."

It struck me that this was also not bad advice for any mother, caught up in all the mess that small children bring. I wondered whether 'tidying away all the toys half a dozen times a day' counted as one achievement or six? Reflecting back over the previous couple of days I realised that I'd actually accomplished an awful lot.

"I think I've had my fair share of major events for a while now. Yesterday Eleanor came down with a fever. Thankfully she's fine, just dosed up on Calpol."

I had told myself not to panic, but fever could mean malaria. Of all the reasons I didn't want to be here, that came at the top of the list. Fever could also mean flu, or a virus, or a host of other problems, but malaria can be treated if caught early enough. Of course, Stephen was at work and I had rushed down to the clinic alone with my baby girl, fearful for her life.

Life crises don't seem to induce tears in me until they have passed. Panic-stricken though I was, I knew I had to keep a cool head; but when the blood film proved negative, I wept with relief. This wretched move

Table talk

to Africa had brought yet another challenge that I needn't have had to face. By the time Stephen was home from work Eleanor was fully drugged up and sleeping the virus off.

"I'm glad she's OK," Richie said. "I gather there was no water earlier either?"

"Just after lunch. Well, probably much of the day, but it was only after lunch that it became apparent. It wasn't the best way to calm my nerves."

I was alerted when Precious said there was no water to wash the clothes. I was trying to give Eleanor some Calpol, and Matthew chose the same moment to scald himself on the hot water coming directly from the boiler. Not ideal, since there was no cold to cool him off.

"I'll notch it up as my achievement for the day," I said. "All the family still alive."

◈

"She's eight years old but weighs just eight kilograms," Stephen exclaimed. "Eight kilograms! That's what she should have weighed at twelve months."

He shook his head sadly.

"What can you do for her?" asked Richie.

"Much the same as for all the others. We cure the infection that brought them in, we feed them, give them milk to build up some weight and strength to resist the next infection that comes their way, then send them home."

"And then?"

"Then? Well, nothing. The malnutrition isn't solved, is it? Just the infection. For a brief period they've come into hospital and been able to get food. But when they get home…" Stephen shrugged his shoulders. "Still no money, still no food. In fact, even less money, because they've just had to pay for the treatment at and transport to the hospital. It is little wonder that they don't come until it is absolutely necessary."

"And therefore the mortality rate is high." Richie finished his thoughts for him.

The subject of how to improve the mortality rate on the ward was something Stephen had mentioned before. The problem of malnutrition was endemic. In large families with few wage earners (and traditionally the first food on the table went to the man of the house) the youngest were at high risk as the food wouldn't go round. If there was any meat at all it would have been eaten long before their turn. Often they would just live off water (which may not be safe) and the staple nshima. Most babies were breastfed, but when weaned they fell to the end of the queue, and if there wasn't enough food for the mother either then even breastfed babies were at risk of insufficient nutritional intake.

That Zambians viewed UTH as the last resort was frustrating, a self-perpetuating spiral towards disaster. Often they only went when all else had failed, be it witchdoctors, potions or clinics, and they were therefore more likely to be close to death. The majority of people in the hospital died so it was thought that you only go to UTH to die, and thus the vicious circle perpetuated.

"At least it looks like I'll never be short of severely malnourished children for my research," he concluded with a wry smile. Changing the topic he asked, "How's life at EFZ, Richie? Any progress?"

"I think we have filed a few pieces of paper today," he joked. "More seriously, it looks like our financial controller is leaving. Something of a headache, as he is actually very reliable."

"You should apply," Stephen teased me.

I gave him a silencing look, but Richie had picked up interest.

"Are you an accountant?"

I swallowed my food. "Well, yes, technically. But I haven't worked for a long time, not since Matthew was born."

"Are you interested in working?"

I didn't know. I was struggling to get to grips with living in this strange country, let alone working. Then again, now I had Sherry and Precious running the house, perhaps I should exercise my brain a bit more.

"There's a lot to do at the moment," I prevaricated. "Do you know where's best to buy some comfy chairs? I was too slow to get them from that family that's leaving next week."

Being the mother of two young children, I was well versed in the art of distraction and the conversation moved on; but a seed had been planted. I couldn't sit around and do nothing for two years. Could I possibly go back to work?

THE DOCTOR'S HOUSE CALL

We had two carpentry failures under our belts so far. The case of the dining chairs was one. It was obvious we should have had the courage to insist on straight legs. They also would have been better made without the random nails we could see in the seats of the chairs. Nevertheless, their workmanship remained of a much higher quality than that of the single bed from the carpentry co-operative. Despite Stephen ordering it three months before we arrived, it had clearly not been started until he chased up on it, and even then it had taken weeks to be completed. The wood was rough, poorly sanded and questionably varnished, thus catching the mosquito netting at every turn. When in place we discovered the frame was six inches wider than the mattress.

The doctor's house call

It was used because we had no choice. After a brief moan about it, followed by a discussion about where on earth we should go to get the other beds we needed, Precious let slip (delightfully gently) that her brother, Daniel, was a carpenter. She took us to see a bed he had made for Tanvir. It was beautiful: perfectly smooth and well-varnished. Daniel, therefore, was busy with an order for a cot for Eleanor.

But now there was a problem. Precious' niece was not well. "She's got a white tongue," Precious said. Would Stephen be able to have a look at her?

She asked this in a shy, hesitant manner, but with a quiet confidence that we would oblige.

Stephen came home early from work and, leaving the children with Sherry, we went to Garden compound to meet Daniel and his daughter, Mutende. Daniel smiled like his sister, with a cap on his head and a pencil behind his ear. We picked him up at his workshop and drove round the corner to his home.

I wasn't strictly needed on the trip but I went along as a show of support for my husband on the one hand and Precious on the other. Besides, I was intrigued to see the girl: even to my non-medic ears 'white tongue' didn't sound good. This was my first chance to see how the local people lived. To date, my interaction with locals had been limited to that of employer, or purchaser (both food and furniture), or observer – watching the gardeners shuffle the leaves around the property or open and close the gate to a honking horn.

Daniel's home was on the edge of the compound, behind the houses on the main road that carried on to the sewage plant. In the city nearly all the houses were made of concrete and roofed with corrugated iron. The best houses fronted the roads; further back their quality deteriorated, many being makeshift, put up in a hurry on a mediocre budget. All too often the concrete was not of sufficient quality and so the breezeblock walls disintegrated and collapsed. So far this was not Daniel's problem, although the outside of the house looked shabby. All around was dust, stone and waste. There were locals passing by, chickens scratching in the dirt and no signs of a plant anywhere.

We entered directly into the main living space. There was another room behind, but the door was firmly shut as a young girl hurried to find Daniel's wife. I was surprised by the space: then again, if you can't afford furniture you would simply have space. The only source of light was the window to the front, scantily covered with wisps of material that had seen better days. Immediately opposite the front door was the kitchen area: a couple of cupboards, piled with cheap pots and pans. There was a stove with a pan of something bubbling away – presumably nshima being boiled in the traditional fashion. On the side was a plastic basin, stacked with items for washing and part-filled with water. A rickety shelf held some basic food, all left open to the elements. This was in complete contrast to our own fastidiousness, putting inside well-sealed Tupperware pots anything that the ants – or even worse cockroaches – might take a fancy to. The smell of boiled food was unappetising and permeated the room.

We were shown over to the sofa and chairs. I might have been uncertain of my purpose in being there but nevertheless I was to be treated as guest of honour. I got the one upholstered chair, a dirty red, worn from years of use. Tentatively I sat down, concerned that I might get bitten by something living in it. In front of me there was a coffee table, shining with the heavy varnish typical of cheap Indian furniture available in the markets.

And on the sofa was Mutende. She was lying down, head propped by a cushion. Even I could tell she was

The doctor's house call

sick. Her eyes protruded from her sunken face, she clearly had no energy and she looked skinny. Her mother sat by her feet and Precious acted as translator between her and Stephen.

I'd never seen Stephen at work before. He sat quietly with the family, said hello to Mutende and smiled. He was warm and encouraging, asking gentle, simple questions to try to establish the cause and duration of her illness.

"How long has she been like this?"

A month.

"What about her appetite? How much does she eat?"

Not much, it turned out.

"What do you feed her?"

Nshima. Porridge. Relish.

"Have you taken her to a doctor? What did he say?"

Yes, they took her to the local clinic. They said she had anaemia. She had been given some tablets. From what Stephen could work out she'd been given anti-malarials for her anaemia, not iron tablets, but they had been encouraged to feed her meat: plenty of it. I glanced around the room, looked at the nshima bubbling on the stove and sniffed the lingering cabbagey smell. No sign of meat: probably outside the family budget. Why would a local doctor prescribe something so inappropriate for her illness, and expect such a family to be able to afford meat?

Stephen looked into Mutende's eyes, took her pulse, felt her throat and looked in her mouth. He prodded her stomach and listened to her chest. He appeared puzzled, pushed his questions again to find out how long she had been ill. Four weeks, a month. When did she go to the doctor? Three, four days ago. After a long, thoughtful pause, Stephen said, "I think she needs to go into hospital, to be seen by a specialist. I'm a little unclear about how the system works here." He looked back at Mutende, then at her parents. "How about I write a letter that you take to the paediatrician tomorrow? When I go into the hospital I'll speak with them, so that they are aware of her, then they will be ready for you when you come."

"Thank you, sir, thank you." The gratitude was effusive. I got a pen from my bag while Stephen found paper in his. The letter written, we took our leave.

The journey home was quiet as we each took in what we had witnessed. I pondered the poverty of the house, the cooking pots bubbling on the stove, the cheap trashy imported furniture, the mysterious 'other room' where I assumed the family slept. I naïvely wondered why Daniel hadn't made himself a beautiful wooden table but, on thinking it through, suspected he never had the excess money to make items for himself and his family.

"The health system here can make you so cross," Stephen said suddenly. "No-one seems keen to actually give a diagnosis. The doctors take your fee and prescribe something – usually anti-malarials. Nothing is said about what is actually wrong. The patient and family are supposed to just trust them, live in faith." I glanced at him, seeing the fury in the set of his jaw. He sighed and continued. "In the UK we are taught to speak about the illness, its diagnosis, its prognosis and the details of any drugs that are prescribed. I guess the level of education is much lower, but still…You'd hope that many people would understand, that they'd be open to learning about their bodies. And what's the use of prescribing drugs a family can't afford? It makes me so angry."

I said nothing, leaving him to his rant, then the quiet as he fumed. The silence lengthened: he was lost in thought about his patient and the healthcare she had available to her.

I took his hand and squeezed. "You OK?"

"Yes," he smiled weakly. Looking straight ahead he spoke quietly. "I think she has leukaemia."

MY LESSON IN ABC

The day was passing quietly at home. Sherry was busy entertaining Matthew and Eleanor. I spent much of my time like an amphibian, trying to keep my body at the right temperature. The shade became too cool as the winter winds whistled round; the sun became too hot. Sitting outside, reading my book, I dodged either the sun or the clouds, moving the chair about every twenty minutes in order to maintain some equilibrium.

Reading was a privilege, a luxury, a holiday treat. I had plucked up the courage to read *The Africa House* by Christina Lamb, which my godmother gave me for my birthday before we came out. It was about Stewart Gore-Browne who fell in love with Zambia and decided to build a little bit of England in it: namely a large manor house called Shiwa Ngandu. The thought of reading anything about Zambia horrified me a few weeks earlier. Sitting in my garden, I wondered whether we ought to get out of Lusaka and see some of this strange land. Perhaps a visit to this red-brick house? And the lake? The hot springs?

The only place to catch the sun in the middle of the day was under the washing line since the rest of the garden was overshadowed by the mulberry tree. So there I was, ducking the dripping clothes as well as the clouds. In its favour, my vantage point was good for nosing at the neighbours: no-one could come in or go out without me noticing. I took a long drink from the glass by my feet and let my thoughts turn to the next event in the day: lunch.

Reluctantly I rested the book on my chair and headed indoors to make a sandwich. Returning I realised that I had to balance book, sandwich, drink and ants. I sighed: my life seemed to be an unending list of bizarre decisions to be made in the face of the complete unknown. I knew there were ants. They were in the soil and I could sometimes see them scurrying around between the blades of grass. If I left my plate on the ground they would come for the crumbs. How they knew so quickly where the source of a few crumbs of food was I could only imagine, although I did think that a heavy china plate on top of their usual route, or even their home, might have had much to do with it.

Could I risk putting the plate on the ground? Would they have preferred the glass of water? How could I balance them both and still save the precious book for reading? My conclusion was that I couldn't put the plate on the ground and risk the ants getting to it before me, so I delicately put down the water, moved the book to the ground, sat down and returned to my drink again.

It should take seconds but somehow every decision like this required deep thought and subtle manoeuvring.

Nothing in Zambia was as straightforward as it should be.

Richie drove up to his flat opposite, waving as he passed me. I waved back, trying not to knock over my food or drink in the process. I really wanted to be engrossed in my book.

A few minutes later he joined me, taking a seat on the grass, leaning against the telegraph pole. *What about the ants?* I thought.

"Hello!" he said.

I looked askance at the bowl on his lap. "Hello! What have you got there?"

"Lunch," he replied, then elaborated. "Muesli. I haven't got long and didn't buy bread. It seemed a good option."

Inadvertently I remembered the joys of being single, of having responsibility to no-one but yourself. Lunch in our house was never cereal. It was usually a sandwich, but every so often, when I felt really daring, it might be eggs or beans and toast. Of course, Eleanor had the most exciting diet: mashed up carrots or swede or apple or a combination of them all. But cereal: that was for breakfast. I smiled.

"What brings you and the cereal out here?"

"I just came to join you," he said.

I was speechless. It was such a lovely thing to do. No-one else was likely to talk to me before Stephen got home from work — well, no adult just for the sake of conversation. The children would demand things and Precious would ask me to move so she could hang up the next lot of washing, but that hardly constituted conversation. I discarded thoughts of returning to my book and concentrated instead on being sociable.

"How's work?" I asked eventually, then immediately chastised myself for such an inane question: are we all defined by what we do? I supposed my alternative was

My lesson in ABC

the weather which, given it was sunny and not going to rain for another three or four months, was limited as a conversation opener.

"Fine," he said. He gave a small laugh and looked to the skies. "Actually, this morning there's been quite an amusing frenzy of activity."

"Really? Frenzy, at EFZ?" Given the general pace of work Richie had spoken of, I found this hard to believe.

"Well, maybe frenzy is too wild a term, but certainly some upset. Boxes have been moved in and out with remarkable speed."

I looked at him quizzically. "Boxes of what?"

He raised an eyebrow, a cheeky glint in his eyes. "Condoms."

"Condoms!" I exclaimed. "At EFZ?"

Richie laughed. "Yes. Despite their deeply Bible-based and quite conservative Christian views, a shipment of condoms arrived today. The staff couldn't get rid of them fast enough!"

"Why were the condoms there in the first place?"

Richie explained. "Leah needs overseas funding for her AIDS projects but many donors will only give money if there is an adherence to the ABC rules."

"ABC?"

"Abstain, Be faithful, use Condoms. It is a globally used acronym to limit the spread of the disease. EFZ only believe in A – could, at a stretch, be sympathetic to B but really: C?! It is completely against their biblical teachings of one man, one woman: man and wife only."

In the month or so that I had been there my head was bursting with newly acquired knowledge on the subject of HIV/AIDS. The disease was a deadly killer, practically wiping out a generation within the nation. "Surely, given the prevalence of the disease, they can see the need that there is for condoms? People aren't necessarily faithful, so surely there should be easy access to condoms – or anything that will prevent the further spread of the disease?"

"Ah, yes, you would think so. But should a Christian organisation be supporting this in any way? Should that be left to other organisations without the same belief system? Are we just compromising our faith?"

It was an interesting argument. Do watered-down beliefs result in a flavourless faith? Or is it too concentrated to begin with: so strong that few are able to stomach the taste?

Richie finished his muesli. "EFZ needed the money, so they found a way round this: they would simply be a conduit for another organisation. That way EFZ still does the amazing social work caring for the families, the sick and the dying, while someone else distributes the condoms. However, you should have seen the minister's face when he walked into his office this morning and found boxes and boxes of condoms stacked up in front of him. His eyes nearly popped out of his head!"

I laughed so much I knocked my sandwich plate to the ground, scattering crumbs for those hungry ants. I had images of dozens of locals scurrying around to hide the condoms – some moving them to a waiting van, closing and locking the doors firmly behind them; others redistributing them around the office, under desks, in drawers, out of sight; and whirling around, a panicking Pastor, demanding the dangerous contraband be moved immediately in case anyone should possibly see it, doing his best to hide the packaging with a threadbare tea-towel and a couple of lever-arch files.

"They've been moved on pretty quickly!" Richie wrapped up his tale, stretched his legs and reached for his empty bowl. "Right! I must be getting back. They'll wonder where I am." He smiled and got up from his grassy seat.

TO HEALTH AND HAPPINESS

It was a week later: a beautiful, sunny afternoon. Sherry was busy pushing Matthew around the compound on his tricycle. Walking through our cool corridor I snuck a look in at my daughter, asleep in her cot. She lay there so peacefully, oblivious to my anxieties. Her very being calmed me down.

She had a blessed life, revolving around sleeping and eating, with a bit of play in between. Eleanor's complaints about anything were rare – or perhaps I'd got a better routine than I had with Matthew. Eating she did particularly well: lots of it, food everywhere. How Precious managed to wash out all those tomato stains by hand in cold water I'll never know.

They were the reason I kept going, she and Matthew. They'd inherited their father's healthy outlook on life: cheerful, optimistic, go-getting. Thank goodness their

In the shade of the mulberry tree

mother's influence was simply on appearance. The thought made me laugh (it's not that great an inheritance!).

I adjusted her blankets, recoiling sharply as she moved – *no! don't wake up!* – then breathed again, as it was merely a stretch, a turn, the continuation of a dream. Even in sleep she had an infectious smile, cheering my low spirits.

I thought of Mutende, in her hospital bed, and of the anxiety that must be filling her parents. Stephen had said that he'd seen her the day before and she was quite cheerful following a course of antibiotics; indeed that she was sitting in bed doing homework. The blood film had taken days to process, the registrar waiting for the consultant professor to give his confirmation. But they'd seen lymphoblasts confirming the leukaemia. Her only hope was chemotherapy, due to start in a month or two's time.

I gazed again at Eleanor, marvelling at how perfect she was. Hearing Matthew bounding in through the front door I tiptoed out of the bedroom, closing the door quietly so as not to disturb my baby's sleep. In the living room I swept Matthew up in my arms and revelled in his joy. He poked my face and tried to tickle me under my chin. I thanked God that I had so much to be grateful for and, whatever I might think of being dragged to Africa, my family were in the peak of health.

∽

I'd had a good day.

I snuggled up to Stephen and reflected on how it wasn't quite so unbearably cold at night any more. Not that I was going to give up the three blankets on top just yet, but at least I was being close to Stephen out of love rather than desperation for bodily heat. July was marching on and Sherry had told me that August would be warm. "The windy month," she said.

The highlight of the day was the evening: an evening out! I'd moaned the other day that I felt trapped by the house, waiting all day for Stephen to finish work then watching him fall asleep early evening. I'd endured nearly two months of this: wouldn't it be nice to go and sample some of the restaurants listed in the Visitor's Guide to Lusaka? To get away from the house and explore a little bit? The drawback had been finding a babysitter, particularly someone I could trust.

Richie came up with the answer, as if we were completely stupid for not having thought of it ourselves. "Why don't you ask Sherry?" he suggested. "I'm sure she'd be glad of the extra money."

I was delighted to have found a way for us to pay our maid a little bit extra for a modicum of work, which also had the added benefit of giving us a social life. The children were usually both in bed and asleep by seven o'clock so her duties were simply to monitor them, make sure nothing untoward happened.

Of course, this evening the schedule was completely thrown. Matthew had played in the bath while I gave Eleanor her final feed. My mind was elsewhere, mentally listing all the things I had to tell Sherry ('just in case…') Eleanor took forever to finish feeding and didn't settle straight away when put in her cot. Matthew played up: Sherry was bathing him and this was new. It meant he could try some new tricks to avoid getting clean and into bed.

I had dashed around, leaving instructions for Sherry. "Eleanor should just sleep through, but if not there is some milk made up in the fridge. Just warm it lightly by putting the bottle in some hot water. Matthew may talk to his teddy for a while but should be no trouble. My mobile number is on the piece of paper by the telephone. Don't hesitate to call if there's any problem."

"Yes, Madam. No problem!" Sherry beamed.

I scrabbled around anxiously for a pen.

"Come along, Catharine," Stephen called. "Richie's waiting."

"OK!" I shouted back. Turning again to Sherry I said, "Are you sure you're all right? Anything you need?"

"No, Madam, I'm fine. Please – go!"

Once again the only one fretting about this whole event was me. Sherry had done this many times before and was completely in control. Matthew loved the extra attention, Eleanor was already fast asleep. Stephen was much better at making the decision to trust, and then to let it be. I was mother hen, anxious, running about, protective of my chicks.

I said a cheery goodbye, kissed my son on the cheek and dashed out the door. Once in the car I allowed myself to unwind and finally look forward to the evening ahead.

Our destination had been the Engineer's, a pub on Cairo Road in the centre of town. Tonight was the monthly pub quiz and I was joining 'The Wooden Spooners'. The team had met up in March when Stephen was visiting and he'd been able to catch the inaugural pub quiz. Their team name had been remarkably prophetic. This evening's aim was to do better than last place.

I stretched out in bed, remembering the balmy night, the smoky pub atmosphere, the 'Britishness' of it all. There were two pop music rounds, which pretty much finished us off. Clicking fingers and humming tuneless tunes were our only weapons at trying to guess what song the written lyrics came from. We played our joker on the 'human body' round, quite rightly expecting

Stephen the doctor to pull us through. I smiled with pride recalling his ability to answer all the questions: the anatomy prize at university did have some long-term benefits after all.

We weren't last, though were by no means first. But most importantly I had had a fantastic time: relaxing over a drink, eating a good meal and laughing with friends. For a couple of hours I had forgotten where I was and the day-to-day challenge to survive Africa.

Stephen rolled over and put his arm across my body. I smiled and snuggled down into his cosy embrace. I was so lucky to have him. He had been so supportive of me, of my fears and worries about being in Africa, a perpetual shoulder to cry on. He had gently encouraged me to get out and about. He hadn't complained about the number of hot chocolates I'd bought at the bakery or the increased food bill as I sought a Western diet. He hadn't laughed when I'd backed out of doing something for a petty reason nor criticised the way I spent my days. He had been there for me unfailingly and I was eternally grateful. Without him, this adventure would simply not be happening.

Content, warm and loved, I fell asleep.

THE BISHOP AND THE PROFESSOR

Soon after our arrival we had decided that our lives would be easier with our own transport. Taxis were cheap, if an adventure in themselves: it was considered a bonus if they had petrol in. More than once Stephen had got halfway to work when the car just came to a halt as the engine was unable to eek more fuel out of the tank on an incline.

We did experiment with hiring a car, at vast expense, for a few days. It was the cheapest that the hire company would offer: a white Citi Golf. It didn't have power steering and I took several attempts to manoeuvre the vehicle into our narrow driveway, avoiding both ditch and hedge. It did serve a purpose –

The Bishop and The Professor

if only to define that we didn't want *that* one but we did need something.

This explains why I was now being driven around the city by a bishop in a Mitsubishi Pajero. He was in the process of selling his car to me. We had to go to the police station, the vehicle licensing offices, the insurers and, for some unknown reason, an office on Kabalenga Road. The last stop had nothing to do with our car purchase, but completed the bishop's business for the day.

It was going to be our second vehicle: the family car, the four-by-four to take us out of the city and on excursions into the countryside. Stephen went through all this bureaucratic paraphernalia on his own when purchasing his car. He'd discovered that a Russian professor at the hospital was selling his Toyota Starlet: perfect for tootling around town (where the roads were usually surfaced) and for Stephen to trek from the laboratory where he worked to the paediatric wards where he saw his patients – a twenty-minute walk from one end of the hospital to the other.

Already the cars had become known as The Professor and The Bishop.

I enjoyed being up high in the car, able to look out at everyone, getting glimpses over the high walls. We drove up Los Angeles Boulevard (formerly known as Saddam Hussein Boulevard), overtaking a broken-down minibus. Buses were prone to many of the same problems as the taxis: running out of fuel, rigorous police checks, cracked windscreens and bits of the vehicle hanging off at peculiar angles. Many of them had terrible wheel alignment, with the front wheels a good foot askew of the rear two. Combine these faults with the bumpers fixed on with duck tape and doors held at jaunty angles and you begin to get an idea of the road-worthiness of public transport.

In the shade of the mulberry tree

The Bishop's secretary explained about some of the cars we passed. "That is an embassy vehicle: CD on the number plate indicates the embassy. Each is a different number. Britain," she said, rolling her Rs, "Britain is number 1, the United States is number 2." I laughed and expressed my delight that we came first, ahead of the Americans at something. Already I anticipated the family entertainment as we worked out which embassy had which number. The only other number the secretary could remember was 34. "Angola," she said, shaking her head and tutting quietly. "Very bad drivers."

The condition of the ambassadorial vehicles was a complete contrast to that of the public transport. Around town I saw plenty of other BMWs and Mercedes, purchased new by the wealthy, which glistened and gleamed along the dusty streets, clearly washed before and after each journey by the gardener, boldly declaring the personalised number plate. For the rest of us mere mortals the closest to 'new' was importing second-hand from Japan. The registration plates had a labelling system that gave you an indication of the age of a vehicle, but only since the date of import. By registration plate The Bishop was only about two or three years old but, being a 1992 model, in reality about eleven years old; The Professor was a comparative youngster aged four.

Sitting in the back I watched the erratic driving all around. I squirmed as a bus driver quickly overtook, then cut across and pulled into the bus stop. Immediately the indicator went on, signalling the driver's intention to come out again. The Bishop just drove straight past, shaking his head. He pointed out a defect in a taxi in front. "That won't get through a police check with only one reflective strip on the bumper." The strapping to hold the bumper on or the shopping bags substituting for a window were of less concern: the police had specific boxes to tick.

From my vantage point in the back of the car I could watch the traffic on the road ahead. Other drivers' ability to weave through traffic was amazing: there was something spectacular about sitting in a traffic jam at the top of a hill and watching a car dodge into all the half-gaps ahead until it reached the lights half a mile further on.

My journey ended at the Bishop's house to leave him (and a large cheque) before I drove myself home. Most of our city driving had been on good quality roads: tarmacked and smooth. The Japanese government had recently completed the reconstruction of the Great East Road, which made the journey from the east side of town, including the airport, into a comfortable trip. Elsewhere, the quality of roads was variable. It helped if you lived on the same road as an embassy or ambassadorial residence, particularly if that country was funding any of Zambia's road building programme. However, lots of roads had clearly not been re-surfaced for many years and were potholed throughout. The journey to the Bishop's home showed the gradual deterioration, from dodging potholes to skirting the kerbsides and grassed roadside verges.

Driving carefully home, it was clear The Bishop had good suspension and I gently bounced along. I was anxious in case I had to stop at a police check. I was on my own now and, although I was confident everything was in order, I started to worry that they would pick something I didn't know about. Would they be right, or would I?

I felt like I was driving a tank as I turned the car into our driveway, taking two attempts to make the manoeuvre perfectly. This luxurious vehicle had to last us a long time. I switched it off and jumped out of the car, waiting for the engine to cut. The Bishop had warned me of the timer designed to let the engine cool down and let the turbo cooler work. I pressed the red button on the key fob and a satisfying 'ping, pong' beep indicated it was all locked.

Sherry had come out and smiled. "Nice car," she said, nodding in appreciation. I felt strangely comforted: if she thought it OK then it probably was. Proud of my day's adventure I headed inside to file the sheaf of paperwork the purchase had produced and to find the *Lonely Planet Guide to Zambia*.

Now we could make proper plans to venture out of town, to leave Lusaka and travel into the unknown.

LOWER ZAMBEZI

"Happy Birthday, Daddy!"

Matthew scrambled onto the bed, waking his bleary-eyed father. I set the mug of tea on the bedside table and gave Stephen a quick kiss, but all his attention was needed for his excitable son, desperate to open presents: there was little chance of Stephen opening anything himself with all that youthful energy available to help. I tied back the mosquito net and settled down with the more placid Eleanor on the other side. At ten months she hadn't yet discovered the joy of ripping open the parcels in front of her.

Matthew's gift was a lavender plant, to be placed in the ground outside our bedroom window. It was part of my one-woman war against malaria (focused solely on my own family). Someone at baby group had said

In the shade of the mulberry tree

mosquitoes don't like strong smells (being one of the reasons that the repellents work so well) and recommended planting strongly scented plants outside bedroom windows. I had no evidence of the efficacy of this but I had enough gardening knowledge to be concerned about the lavender's potential for growth. The 'flowerbed' outside was unfertilised soil barely a couple of inches deep, completely shaded by the roof overhang and jacaranda trees.

As he was handed the undisguised present Stephen asked, "Matthew, do you know what this is?"

"Happy-birthday-Daddy!" he replied, overcome by excitement. Immediately the plant had a name.

There was no time, though, for any planting. We were taking advantage of Stephen's birthday to go on a big adventure: we were travelling out of town.

I had booked us into a lodge on the Lower Zambezi for the weekend, about a couple of hours' drive from Lusaka. The travel agents (whom I thought I trusted) recommended it and the price was not extortionate. Besides, Stephen deserved a birthday treat and if I had to live here I was determined to see as much of Zambia as was practical.

Organising our departure took us nearly to lunchtime, but at last the children were strapped in, books, sweets and other diversions were put in easy reach, The Bishop was filled with diesel and we were ready to go. Sherry was there to wave goodbye.

"Take care of my babies," she called.

I whipped round to look at her. "Whose babies?" I retorted, then broke into a smile and laughed. "Of course I will!"

At last we left. Directions appeared simple: we could see from the map that basically we had two left turns, one just past Kafue towards Chirundu, then again at Chirundu (the border town with Zimbabwe). After that the lodge had told us to follow the road until we saw a sign for them on the right-hand side.

We braced ourselves for a long journey with young children. Thankfully they were as interested as we were by the sights of driving through Lusaka: into the city down Independence Avenue past the Freedom Statue, skirting the edge of Cairo Road, abiding by the incredibly slow speed limits for three nearly empty lanes of traffic as we headed south and away from home. I was driving, with Stephen pointing out novelties as we passed.

"Did you see the concrete elephants?"

"What's that turning for?"

"Look how tall that wooden giraffe is – would it fit in the back?"

Eleanor drifted off to sleep, softly cushioned in her car seat. Matthew turned to reading books. I slowed down for the bridge crossing the Kafue River: a long structure spanning the river whose waters had spread out over the flat country around. The light sparkled on the sluggish water, promising more.

Next came a police check, beside a large sign telling us 'Do not bribe the police officials'. The beautifully kept road became a series of mounds and bumps as we slowed down. Ahead we could see the mirage effect of heat rising from the road and Stephen concluded that the road must simply melt and reshape with all the heavy lorries on it pulling to a halt.

"Look at that one," he said, pointing to a large articulate coming the other way. It was laden high with goods, buckling under the strain. It had become a sport for us, to find the worst vehicle on the road, and this one was winning the 'precarious loads' category. Lorries and trucks usually beat the buses: the cockeyed axles were a constant amusement as we drove along behind them. Top that with some weighty cargo (or better still, some loose livestock) and an exhaust belching black smoke and it was a wonder that they moved at all.

The police check passed without problem, as did the ad hoc one a few kilometres further on in Kafue town. It was the left turns that confused. All the maps we had showed the T1 going from Lusaka to Livingstone with our road to Chirundu as a branch off. In practice there was a sign sponsored by the local sugar producers indicating a turn right for all destinations to the Victoria Falls: our route had right of way. I wondered how many tourists missed the sign and cheerily drove on, oblivious to the error of their way.

Perhaps not many, as once past the few houses surrounding the junction the road markedly deteriorated. At that point I assumed any sensible tourist would question the route: we certainly did.

But we were on the right road. Our speed slowed dramatically as we dodged the holes. We even started to make mental notes of what we could see on the other side so that we could prepare for them on the way home. This exercise was quickly abandoned as neither of us had memories that well trained. World champions would struggle to make that many associative links. The difficulties were exacerbated by long stretches of good road, which suddenly fell apart. Thankfully there was little traffic so we could 'overtake' the potholes.

When not staring intently at the road, Stephen was able to take in the glorious countryside around. It had become more mountainous and the hills were covered with changing trees that were creating a beautiful patchwork of greens, reds, orange and gold. In parts, new growth broke through, bright fresh green, striving for sunlight away from the more mature trees. Stephen pointed out flame creepers winding their way to the top of the canopy and bursting into scarlet flower.

"It's amazing," I said, awed by the colourful display. "I'm surprised the plants are in flower. The rains are still months away – at least two. Sherry said possibly three or four. Don't they need the rain for growth, to allow the flowers to bloom?"

"I guess rains are also needed for the seeds to germinate and grow – so perhaps it makes sense to flower now, so that the seeds are ready for the rainy season. Presumably that helps the reproduction."

"It sounds logical, but how on earth do they know that the rains are coming, two months or more away? What triggers this burst of flower after five months of no water?"

Matthew (uninterested in local botany) demanded that we turn the tape over and please could he have another book and were there any more biscuits? We resumed parental mode: anything for peace so that we could enjoy the journey. The drive was stunning, winding through the hills at the edge of the Central African high plateau that most of Zambia sits on, before falling down to the Zambezi River at the bottom. We blindly followed an articulated lorry carrying tonnes of metal along the road, precipitous drop on one side, rock falls on the other.

Suddenly, going up a slight incline, the lorry stopped. I did too. Then I realised that I had to get past: he was going nowhere. The bendy road meant that I could see no further than the driver's cab. Anything could have come round the corner, easily coasting downhill at the 80 kph that I had been doing, and smack straight into me. The driver's arm gesticulated wildly out of the window. I had to trust that this meant I could overtake and that there was nothing coming the other way. It was so unclear that it could equally have meant 'whatever you do, don't overtake'. Heart in stomach, I took a deep breath and edged past.

At Chirundu we had another left turn. Irrationally fearful of reaching the border and not being able to avoid entering Zimbabwe, I turned a junction too early. It was obvious that this was the wrong route and I was forced into a three-point turn on the dirt road. Being new to me I was still uncertain as to where The Bishop's tank-like physique began and ended, so my three points became many more. Moving cautiously back onto the main road, ever closer to the border post, we found another left turn.

I was more convinced but the first stretch had become a single lane road in the middle of nearly a kilometre of HGVs parked either side. Alongside all the articulated lorries my robust four-wheel drive felt puny and I had to give way to impatient truckers eager to reach the border. Previous trucks had destroyed whatever there was supposed to be in the way of a road and I nervously navigated The Bishop through the bumps and turns.

"Are you sure this is the right way?" I queried.

"Yep. Positive." Stephen's words were more confident than his voice.

Past the lorries, then some housing and stretching out in front of us was not tarmac but a clear, wide road of what looked like compacted gravel. No signs. No indication of where we were or where we were going. There was just a roadside stall in front of a small blue house.

"Are you still sure?"

He didn't feel there was an alternative. There weren't that many arterial roads in Zambia and so the final stretch of our journey was to be on this: a good piece of dirt road.

Dust flew up, coating The Bishop with a fine orange layer. The high clearance vehicle proved its value as we clambered over rocks and stones that protruded from the road surface. By now Eleanor had woken and Matthew was fed up. All our negotiating skills had been utilised, all bribery exhausted.

"Not long to go now!" I chirruped merrily. After all, in comparison with the two-and-a-half-hour stint we had just done, the distance left on the map was negligible.

However, my timing had not taken into account two important factors. Firstly, that the dirt road would slow me down as I was scared of damaging our precious new vehicle, and secondly, we had to cross the Kafue River.

Between Chirundu and the Lower Zambezi National Park lie two rivers: the Kafue and the Chongwe. We had crossed the Kafue once, by the police check. An hour later we had nearly completed a 'U' and had to cross the river again. We came to the river blind, mounting the brow of a hill and braking sharply on the steep descent.

Out of nowhere there were people: pedestrians wishing to cross the river and children playing in the dirt of the roadside. Women were washing their clothes down by the water and the men stood around, nonchalantly, chewing their sticks and watching the world go by.

When we'd last seen it, the Kafue was a lazy, languid river ambling its way through the flats. Here it was fast and deep, much narrower and slightly choppy. And there was no bridge. Instead, at the far side of the river, was a metal raft hung on what appeared to be a piece of rope. The wire was stretched across the river and we watched as a vehicle got on at the other side and then the pontoon was wound back to our bank.

All too soon it was our turn. Somehow, I was expected to drive The Bishop onto this device. My uncertainties about the size of my new vehicle were magnified ten-fold. What if I didn't get the wheels onto

In the shade of the mulberry tree

the twin metal strips set down for me to drive on? Surely they were too thin for my tyres? It all looked most precarious: why should I trust a boat that was only prevented from floating away by its attachment to a bit of string – strong, metal string, I grant you – but nevertheless the absence of any sign of a motor did not instil confidence.

I put the car into first gear and gingerly crept away from the security of land and onto the pontoon, constantly being hurried on by the ferryman and his many local advisors.

Then, at the point of no return, Matthew started screaming, and nothing Stephen or I could say would stop him.

PONTOON PEACE

Matthew screamed and screamed and screamed.

Neither of us could guess what was suddenly so incredibly wrong. We were trapped in the car, half on the pontoon, half off. There were no insects buzzing about, nobody had been up close to the car and he could barely see the pontoon ahead. Stephen turned round in his seat, stroking Matthew's leg, offering words of comfort, but to no avail.

The wailing did nothing to ease my nerves about driving The Bishop onto the raft. Eventually I was able to stop and Stephen leapt out to rescue Matthew from his misery.

The pair of them stood with the locals on the deck of the pontoon while Eleanor and I remained in the car. They saw at first hand the mechanism responsible for getting us from one bank to the other. It was one man's job to turn a handle, thus lengthening the chain behind us and shortening the one in front, slowly pulling us over to the other side. When full the pontoon could take three vehicles plus numerous passengers, so the amount of strength required to haul a fully-laden boat across must have been immense.

At the other side I drove off the pontoon alone, save for Eleanor babbling happily behind me, and I pulled over to wait for my foot passengers to walk up the bank. As he resumed his seat in the back Matthew was calm, seemingly back to normal. All I could think was: *What's going to happen on the way back?*

Not much further on we were faced with loose earth spread across the road, a clear pair of tyre tracks indicating our route, or that of the oncoming traffic, and various criss-crossings over the mud. Unaccustomed to the additional grip that a four-wheel drive gave over and above that of a city hatchback, I drove slowly and came face-to-face with what appeared to be a squashed tractor: one that had met some terrible accident from the side, front wheels a good half-metre askew of its rear.

"Wins the prize for worst wheel alignment yet," Stephen said. It was worse than any minibus or taxi that we had seen so far and, indeed, unlike any other vehicle we had seen before. We had to assume that it was supposed to be there since the shallow scoop at the front, most like a snowplough at a twenty-degree angle, shovelled the soil along purposefully. The driver waved as I overtook.

At an unexpected fork in the road there were some signs for lodges in the Lower Zambezi National Park and, not long after, a wooden notice announcing our lodge. We pulled up on the gravel and stopped, allowing the engine to cool. Only an hour-and-a-half later than everyone expected, we finally made it to our destination.

I was exhausted. The state of the roads (combined with Matthew's screaming fit) had shaken me as much as the car. I sat and stared at the greenery around me, enjoying the peace that came with the engine switched off, realised that I was very thirsty and wondered what time the bar opened. I also remembered we needed to slather ourselves in mosquito repellent.

"Is this it?" asked Matthew. Stopping the car had pulled his attention away from a book. Eleanor gurgled with delight.

"Yes, we are here," I said with a smile. Looking across I saw in Stephen's eyes that the joy of a new adventure far outweighed the exhaustion of the journey.

Our peace was brought to an abrupt halt by the arrival of a team of men in khaki.

"Welcome to Kasanka!" the white man called. "Come, come and have a seat."

We made to get our luggage from the boot.

"Don't worry about that," he said. "The men will carry it to your room."

There was a lot of paraphernalia with two young children, even for just a weekend. We were hurried away and I, paranoid as ever, worried about whether everything would make it to our lodgings. To be safe, I ensured the passports were with us rather than the staff.

We were taken to the main meeting place, a large thatched building, open to three sides. As we walked along the path I saw the river. It was fast flowing but had the calming silence of water. I quickly felt at ease, delighted to discover that we were staying in such a beautiful place. It was stunning with tall trees shading the paths and green grass stretching down to the banks of the river.

In the shade of the mulberry tree

"Please, please, take a seat."

We were shown to some chairs and our host, a cordial Italian who had just completed building the six-chalet site, took our passports to complete the relevant registration forms. I told myself not to panic as I watched our identification disappear into an office out of sight. Meanwhile we got a drink – cold, wet, refreshing. We were told that tea, coffee (proper Italian stuff – what luxury!) and biscuits were always available in this area. Beyond it I could see a substantial terrace stretching out towards the river.

The initial delight in the peace and solitude flipped to fear as a thought crept in: how would the other guests cope with our children? At their age it was difficult to control bouts of crying or exuberance, neither of which would please someone else who was trying to escape from noise. I asked one of the gentlemen when he returned our passports.

"There is no-one else tonight; maybe a couple tomorrow," he said. Relief flooded through me. I sat back with my water, Matthew with a Fanta, Stephen with a Diet Coke and thought: *maybe – just maybe – I got the booking right.*

But most of all we could stop planning and organising, stop sorting the practicalities of our new home, stop the effort of establishing new friends. We could stop – only for a moment, perhaps, but this weekend was just for us.

∽

Darkness had given way to new sounds: hippos grunting in the river, unidentifiable animals howling in the distance, insects chirping away, frogs boldly belching their mating calls. Every sound was magnified thousands of times, so each breaking twig seemed like a falling tree; every whispering grass was expected to herald a new visitor to camp.

"Will they be OK?" I whispered to Stephen, as a man led us along the path back to the communal area. Once dark we were not allowed to wander anywhere without a scout from the lodge. Our children were asleep in the rondavel which was our home for two nights, being guarded by a camp employee.

"They'll be fine! We're not far away – we'll probably hear them crying ourselves."

It must be a male/female thing, the worry about offspring. I fretted that they'd wake alone, in a dark, strange place, cry for their mother and I wouldn't be there. Either the guard would peer in, which would probably upset them even more, or it would take several minutes for me to be chaperoned back to the chalet. Stephen was more relaxed. He recognised that they were already asleep and, based on past performance, were highly unlikely to wake up at all, so why worry?

I had to hold my tongue, keep my anxieties to myself and focus on our meal. As we were the only guests, I was expecting a quiet dinner for two, a rare moment for us to be together and talk about something other than the children. I took a deep breath of the night air and anticipated celebrating Stephen's birthday in style, being waited on at a private table, the river gently lapping at the bank beside us. I might have pulled off the most romantic birthday dinner yet.

Paraffin lamps guided our way, illuminating the terrace and, to our right as we approached, an open fire provided heat as hardwood logs gently smouldered. But instead of the romantic idyll I had conjured up we were shown to a long table set for four. We were to spend the evening making small talk with our host and the manageress. I couldn't help but be disappointed since small talk was all I did with people at present.

In the shade of the mulberry tree

Over three courses of excellent food, the awkwardness wore off. The warm air and excellent company provided for easy, entertaining and informative conversation.

We learnt about the local village, which had recently had a death by a lion. I wondered how far away that was and whether the lion would come here. I couldn't help but look round, peer into the darkness to see if he was there; but night in the bush is pitch-black and I could only hope he was still satiated from his recent attack.

We learnt about what the lodges all along the river were doing to conserve wildlife while generating money from tourism. It was a difficult balance: encouraging people to come and spend money, yet preventing the deterioration of a unique habitat.

We learnt that the peculiar machine we had seen on the road earlier was a grader, making the dirt road solid and flat again before the main tourist season (we were at the front end of this). After that would come the rains that would return most of the neatly compacted earth to the surrounding bush, by means of force and gravity, and leave the remainder to create a washer-board effect road punctuated by rocks and stones.

Embarrassed by our own assessment of the vehicle, I changed the subject of conversation to the lorry that we'd overtaken on the escarpment.

"Ah, you were lucky," our host said. "It is a dreadful piece of road. I always travel at a distance behind the lorries, ready to go into reverse at any point. As you drive along all you see are the carcasses of lorries abandoned when they've run out of fuel, or have jack-knifed over the edge or across the road, blocking traffic in both directions. There are many sections where the road has been destroyed by burnt out trucks."

We'd certainly noticed our fair share of broken-down vehicles. Few owned red warning triangles, so drivers improvised by laying out branches along the road and wedged the wheels with rocks from the roadside. Then they waited, though I could never work out who would be coming to rescue them. We caught a couple of drivers hiding beneath the trucks: sheltered from the heat, but in a mighty precarious position.

"It is the most notorious piece of road in the country," our host continued. "On the escarpment you have to be prepared for anything."

It was the only road from Chirundu into Lusaka and thus the main arterial route for all goods coming into the country. As a general rule people didn't import along the Livingstone road, through Botswana, but brought all their South African goods via Zimbabwe instead. Presumably the roads through Zimbabwe were much better, or shorter, or the customs tariffs were less onerous. Whatever, the escarpment had to be negotiated and heavy loads on unsafe lorries made for many casualties and fatalities en route. We felt more grateful than ever that we had survived overtaking the lorry, and resolved to be more careful on our journey home.

∽

After our sumptuous dinner we were escorted back to our rondavel, the path illuminated by a few kerosene lamps and our guide's torch. I kept an eye out for the lion, of course, and Stephen was proven right: there hadn't been a whisper out of our children since we'd left them. We tiptoed around them and into bed, hushed by the blanket of the African night. To us safari novices the silence was quite unnerving: was there a creature close by that might attack us, eat us all up? I was filled with curiosity. However I was also filled with food and quickly fell into a deep sleep.

In the middle of the night I woke. Something had roused me. More alert to the sound, I recognised that it wasn't my children. This noise was coming from further away.

There was a rustling sound. No, more than that: I could hear shuffling, branches breaking, chomping. Something was out there. Something big, something hungry, something I didn't want to meet just now…but I did want to know what that 'something' was…

I raised my head from the pillow. Everyone appeared to be fast asleep. "Stephen," I whispered loudly. There was a mild grunt, which I recognised as 'OK, I'm vaguely acknowledging that you are awake and I am not, and that you want to talk but really I am asleep and small bomb blasts are unlikely to make any difference to the conversation,' so I got up and peeked out from behind the curtained window.

It was pitch black. There was little moonlight and I began to understand just how dark night could be. I could not see a thing except a solitary lamp near reception, all other lights from the camp now extinguished. The fresh night air blew through the cracks making me shiver. The munching continued but I could not make out what creature was eating his way through the vegetation in the hollow beside our chalet.

I wanted it to be an elephant. All my life I'd had a fascination with elephants and it was my secret hope that at some point while I was in Zambia I would get a chance to see one living in the wild. I was hampered by not having a torch (note to self: *bring torch on next trip*) and briefly I considered going out onto the veranda for a better view. Better judgement prevailed. I had to give up. Reluctantly, I crept back into bed. Elephant spotting would have to be kept for another day.

AN ISLAND WALK

We had confused our safari hosts.

We arrived late. We required babysitting duties. I was vegetarian. All that would, you'd think, be enough, but not from us.

We were on holiday. That meant, in our minds, rest and sleep. It does not mean being woken at 6 am to go on a safari ride. Our hosts were politely confused as, in their minds, that was the reason for coming here. Over our (late) breakfast they asked us what we'd like to do that day. Stephen and I had given little thought to this. All we knew was that we wanted to see animals: lots of them. I asked what the options were.

"Well, you can go on a game drive, but I'm not sure what you will see. The sun is up now and it will be difficult to find animals. We are over two hours' drive from the start of the National Park. This is a GMA –

In the shade of the mulberry tree

Game Management Area – so there are animals, but they are not so well protected." We could tell from his demeanour that he was not at all certain that we would benefit from a game drive. He offered an alternative. "What about the river? Would you like to go fishing?"

Stephen and I looked at each other. As a vegetarian, I was not keen on fishing at all. I remembered the only other time we'd gone fishing together, on our honeymoon. Back then Stephen only managed to catch a solitary small, white, tropical fish barely ten centimetres long after hours of trying.

"I don't think so," I said.

"What about a walk on the island?"

"The island?" I queried.

Our host pointed to trees that I had presumed to be the other side of the river. "We can go and see what we can find there."

So we had confused our host with a desire to see animals at a time of day when they would be hiding from the sun (mad dogs and Englishmen came to mind); we had dismissed fishing in the Zambezi River; and now, for a wildlife walk, I proffered my sandals as stout footwear and asked whether we could bring the children. The inappropriate sandals were hesitantly agreed to; the children were offered alternative entertainment.

"They can stay here. There are a couple of girls who will look after them."

I could understand his viewpoint. Young children created risks by their own unpredictability – the desire to run around or run off – and also by their crying or screaming, which would either scare wildlife away or be welcomed as supper by the more carnivorous beasts.

As I stepped into the boat it was not the children I was most concerned about: it was me. I pretended that I was really very happy about floating away when it was

An island walk

known there were crocodiles on the banks and in the water. Leaving the children *was* a minor concern (after all, I had promised Sherry I would look after her babies). As we chugged away from the shore, I waved to them both: Eleanor was being cuddled by a maid and Matthew waved confidently back, before running off towards the swimming pool. Their concern was significantly less than mine.

I turned to view the island. *This is going to be a positive experience*, I told myself. *I will not worry. It is adventurous, fun, something you can never do back home.* I took Stephen's hand. As with all my Zambian experience, I wouldn't have done it without him.

⁂

After an hour walking in the late morning sun I was feeling the heat and we hurried to sit down in the shade by a small lagoon. Four months into the dry season there was not a lot of water left but it was cooling to rest under the trees for a few minutes. I was certain that some water and a few moments' rest would pick me up, but our guide insisted on giving me a rehydration drink, which tasted utterly disgusting.

Up to now the walking tour had been unspectacular. I came to see animals, especially elephants, and we had not seen a single creature, except for termites, and most of those were hidden deep inside their mounds. Our guide was very knowledgeable about all the plants we passed, describing their medicinal and other properties, and had pointed out several birds flying past. However, that was not what I wanted to see.

We had seen evidence of larger life forms, though, in footprints and droppings. The elephant dung filled me with false hope. Found regularly during the walk, it was totally dry: just straw-like strands formed into cylindrical lumps. The guide explained how nature cleaned up after itself, with dung beetles who, as their name suggested, survived on deposits, shaping bits up into balls and rolling it away to be buried or eaten. Together with the termites, the beetles were largely responsible for the recycling of the animal manure so that the ground was clear and fertile.

I was less excited by the wonders of nature and more by the logical conclusion that the existence of elephant dung meant the existence of elephants to deposit it. Elephants were one of the few enticements that Africa held before coming here. With every fibrous cake we stepped over I hoped to see a large, grey beast striding out of the bushes.

Yet the first one I saw, the one flanking me as I stared at the lagoon sipping at a bottle of water, was merely a skull.

"Is this an elephants' graveyard?" Stephen asked our guide.

Sadly, no. A massive bull elephant with enormous tusks had been 'headhunted' by poachers and, despite all the best efforts of the lodge owners along the riverside, they got through the defences and killed the beast. The ivory was worth more than the peaceful life of a beautiful creature.

I don't know whether it was the shady peace of the lagoon or the powers of the rehydration drink, but after a few minutes I was refreshed enough to face the walk back. The guide took his time to explain more about termites and their symbiotic relationship with trees. Termites are completely destructive, turning a good piece of wood into dust in a matter of hours. Even concrete is not safe from their attack.

"Termites eat trees, developing a termite mound near the foot of their food source. Eventually, as the mound grows and the colony increases, the termites will cut off any nutrients that are reaching the branches and the whole tree will collapse and die. See – here!"

He stopped us beside a fallen tree trunk, dwarfed by a rust-coloured hillock of earth. "The termite mound itself is very hard, rock-like, protecting the termites in a warm cocoon." He knocked at it with his knuckles, returning a deadening thud, then kicked it to prove how solid their home was. The tree trunk was crumbling away at the edges. He snapped some off and rubbed it to dust between thumb and fingers.

"A dead tree: a banquet for the termites."

"So, termites are not good news for trees then," I said.

"We-ell," he responded, "it's not all bad. The mound may be rock solid but they have to come outside to reach their food. They scuttle up, eat the wood and retreat back home. When they come to the surface they are picked at by birds. For the tree, when alive, this is advantageous, as the birds' droppings around the trunk will help fertilise."

"But still: the tree is dead," I pointed out.

"Yes, but the mound is increasingly rich and fertile: a wonderful concoction of soil, fertiliser and the aeration work of the termites. Any seeds that can get through a chink in the rock-like superstructure will appreciate the soil for germination and growth. When the tree dies there is rapidly an end to food for the termites and they will therefore seek another place to set up home. With the termites gone, the mound grows weaker and it is easier for seeds to get through the holes. They can germinate, grow freely and become established." He paused, and pointed to a sapling growing at a wonderful angle from a hump of soil a few metres away. "Many new trees grow out of termite mounds," he concluded.

The lime green leaves of the young tree shone against the brilliant blue sky. There was no breeze to

In the shade of the mulberry tree

speak of and all I could hear was the gentle hum of insects as they buzzed around in the tropical heat. They were the only things with any inclination to move or expend energy. The sun was almost directly overhead and I was looking forward to getting back to the mainland and to my children, having given up hope of seeing any larger animals. As we were warned, most wildlife took advantage of the heat to hide and sleep and so our attention was redirected to insects, bugs and birds, a fascinating world of their own.

Just as our boat came into view our guide stopped abruptly. "Ssh!" he hissed.

Obediently we fell silent. There were a few birds still hovering above in the midday heat and I could hear leaves rustling. Then, in the midst of all the quiet noise, I heard the sound of a branch breaking behind us.

"There!" Our guide pointed to an open patch of land just below us. From our vantage point on the ridge we could see three elephants eating their way through the sparse shrub land. We turned and quietly watched these amazing animals. They were wary of us, clearly sensing us even from our considerable distance: I guess they did have specialised noses for that. When they were comfortable with our presence they renewed their interest in the vegetation around them, ripping up small bushes and chewing on them.

"Three males," the guide whispered.

"How do you know they're male?" Stephen asked.

"The heads are squarer." A small giggle followed. "Besides, look at the guy in front. Can you see his fifth leg?"

Elephants really are huge.

An island walk

Eleanor had fallen asleep on the rug in the shade of the thatched roof. Matthew, though delighted to see us, was busily engaged with his cars. A quiet lunch (interspersed with half-hearted attempts to persuade Matthew to eat something healthy from the buffet selection) then drifted into a peaceful afternoon. Ever conscious of the burning sun we retreated to the cool rondavel, read books and got out the Lego.

It was wonderful to be away from the constant stress of city life, away from all the confusions of the past two months: the work, the different cultural norms and the exhaustion of repeated small talk as we constantly met new people. We had time to unwind, to rest, sleep and relax. And the setting was magical: gently flowing river, birds and wildlife on your doorstep, clear blue skies and sunshine sparkling in the water. Africa wove her magic over us, a soft blanket of tranquillity and peace, sun-induced laziness infiltrating every bone. Even Matthew was taken in by the environment, comfortable playing alone, repeatedly completing and breaking up his jigsaws. Rarely had a holiday been so relaxing, rejuvenating and refreshing – simply so appropriate and necessary to keep family and life together.

Late afternoon we went for a sundowner cruise. The lodge had a magnificent boat, large enough to accommodate our picnic rug, on which Eleanor could sit and play with her toys and Matthew turned the tartan stripes into roads and highways for his cars. We relaxed and enjoyed the ride, receiving another lesson in Zambian birdlife, seeing many more elephants on the Zimbabwean banks and even some splashing through the water from sand bank to island. We passed a bloat of hippos who eyed us warily, snorting away and swimming past quickly. We were alerted to crocodiles as they slipped into the river: the gentle splash usually being the first sign as they were camouflaged well against the sandy dunes. Gin and tonics in hand, we were the epitome of colonialism, floating downstream as we watched a perfect red African sun setting in the western sky.

SNIPS AND SNAPS

Three months had passed since we arrived in Zambia and it was past time to have my hair cut. The smart, cropped look that my London hairdresser gave me had become a ragged mop and my pride, usually not overly concerned with personal appearance, had taken a battering. It had to be dealt with.

Of course, in the UK I knew what to expect from a cut and blow-dry, even if the cost in London never seemed reasonable. But Zambia was different. There were plenty of barbers being advertised at the roadside and some small buildings beautifully decorated with painted pictures of how your hair could look. My biggest concern, though, was whether anyone would be able to cut a white person's hair.

'White' hair was very different to 'black' hair. In addition, mine was blonde, which made it utterly fascinating to black children. Youngsters loved the chance to sit and touch my hair or my children's: straight, blonde, soft. 'Black' hair was much tougher and infinitely curlier. Many women wore wigs or spent their money on regularly replacing hair extensions. Stephen had told me stories of mothers who could get some enjoyment from the time when their daughters were sick as they could braid the young girls' hair in peace – no distractions, movement or complaints. I was certain that a hugely disproportionate amount of any woman's pay went on hair care, taming the strands into beautiful locks. However mine didn't need braiding, I was not keen on hair extensions and I was certainly not prepared for a wig: I needed nothing more than a simple cut.

At a baby group I had asked the other mothers for advice. It's remarkably difficult to ask a woman where she gets her hair done. I was not sure I received much help. The responses were of moderate use, mainly consisting of 'I had it done while I was home in the summer, but I hear that so-and-so is good...' No-one had been to the salons that I had walked past in Kabulonga or Manda Hill. The only name I was given with any potential was a woman who lived behind a gate on Addis Ababa Road.

Driving up and down the road, I was not able to locate which driveway I was supposed to approach. All the gates looked much the same, none having signs outside and I was not feeling courageous enough to take a chance.

I gave up and tried the boutique in the shopping mall.

"How much is a haircut?"

"Fifty thousand kwacha." Was that a reasonable price? Was I overpaying in local terms? Was it too much of a bargain – would I come out looking like Worzel

Gummidge? Then again, compared to London prices, it was delightfully cheap!

"OK – when can I have it cut?" I took the plunge and decided to make a booking, anxiously peering through to the salon. Not a white person in sight: I was doomed.

I consoled myself with some retail therapy before returning home. I was second in the queue at the lights coming out of Manda Hill, with a good view over the Toyota in front. Tragically this view also meant I was first to see the policemen taking their places in the centre of the junction and, although the lights changed to green, we were stuck for the time being. I groaned. Clearly the President was coming through. I had been in this situation before as periodically the roads were cleared for dignitaries to pass. The best thing to do was put on the handbrake and switch off the engine, wait and watch.

The policeman waved the traffic on the Great East Road with great vigour. I could almost hear him shouting, 'Come on! Come on!' to the bewildered drivers coming from town. He urged them on and past him until he got some sort of message, from his boss no doubt, and called a halt to the speeding flow.

Now the focus changed and all the cars had to be taken off the road. He began to direct the traffic again, this time into the shopping centre. This was no mean feat since we had gone through maybe three changes of lights without moving, so there were vehicles queuing throughout the car park. I'd noticed that drivers had little in the way of patience and so junctions became blocked when cars turned across the road, even if that caused a blockage and meant that no other vehicle could get past.

I was quietly cursing this obstruction to our journey home. Matthew was in the back of the car and a bit fratchety: lunch was high on his agenda.

Along came a police outrider. He zoomed past from our left, waving his arm. This was unusual: they were normally so formal and puffed up by their responsibility as they ensured the road was clear for the President. For whom else would the main arterial road from the airport be cleared? Whenever he travelled the entire populace was moved unceremoniously out of the way so that four lanes of road were clear. This left no chance of hijack or ambush nor any hint of humility as the honoured Head of State rushed about his daily business.

The next bike rider was more exuberant than the first. He was standing up on his motorbike, waving wildly and punching the air. I noted that there were people lining the streets, some even with cameras poised, and felt I had to take back all my uncharitable thoughts about Presidential transport: clearly he was loved and appreciated by his people.

From the left the main cavalcade approached. There was much hooting of horns, more policemen standing on their bikes, waving, whooping. There was one closed, no doubt armour-plated vehicle and then a black limousine, sunroof open and a woman standing with her upper torso out of it. She held aloft a flag in the Zambian colours, material streaming out behind her as she waved to everyone she passed. The noise was tremendous as horns were hooted and people cheered. I was astonished to see that the President's limousine was behind hers, then an array of other vehicles followed (including the Presidential ambulance that always was part of his entourage).

Slowly it dawned on me that this was Cherise: this was the woman who won Big Brother Africa and had been met by the President at the airport on her return home. I was struck by the joy and the pride in her achievements, despite many of the bishops in the country calling for a ban of the programme, claiming it immoral and offensive.

The show was over nearly as soon as it began. Once the convoy was past the next set of lights the traffic policemen disappeared back to the comfort of their offices, allowing the lights to take control once more, while in the car park behind me the drivers resumed their arguments over priority and right of way.

∽

The time had come. Haircut. I was sitting in the reception area reading a South African magazine waiting for my appointment. For moral support I had arranged for Stephen to meet me when it was all over. The magazines were a bit of a privilege given the price of purchasing such glossy overseas publications at the shops. I couldn't really claim that it was upmarket, cultured reading but I hadn't read a magazine for months and when you were starved of such material, 'My husband left me for my poodle' and 'How to lose 10 kg in three days' or 'Seven places to have an orgasm around the house' were remarkably important reads.

I was still anxious about the haircut. A million 'what if…' questions floated around my head. I tried to find a picture of what I was hoping for, although I actually just wanted my hair to look neater, tidier and to be more manageable.

I was called through and explained to the girl (who introduced herself as Juliette) what I would like. She smiled, nodded and said, "No problem!" I wished this allayed my fears completely, but it was what I had come to expect from all Zambians, eagerness to please regardless of the ability to execute.

While my hair was being washed my mind wandered. Was Eleanor eating enough? Should I stop breastfeeding? She didn't seem to be drinking much at the moment nor was she very bothered if I was not around. Who was going to complain more if I stopped – her or me?

And Matthew: why was he having these regular nightmares? Was everything OK at school? He seemed happy enough with his little friends and even had a play date with a boy next week. What could be causing him so much upset, and at such regular intervals?

I fumbled in my pocket for my mobile phone, anxious to ensure I was contactable at all times in case anything went wrong for either of them. Feeling its comfortable bulk I wondered how I was going to cope if – or hopefully when – I got a job. Richie had mentioned my professional qualification and availability to the Executive Director at EFZ but, as a foreigner, employment was not straightforward.

I let out an involuntary sigh. I realised I was bored, most of the time. For the first month I had been busy setting up house. For the second I had enjoyed my false holiday, reading books in the sunshine, going to the café for a croissant and to read the papers. But it had all worn thin. I had no household responsibilities other than to buy the food that we all needed; and little in the way of childcare responsibilities, given the constant availability of Sherry and Precious. *"If all the year were playing holiday, to sport would be as tedious as to work. But when they seldom come, they wished for come,"* as Shakespeare wrote. Holidays are interesting because they are rare. Right now my life was almost constant holiday and the extra time on my hands had allowed tedium to creep in. My little grey cells needed exercising. Something had to happen to ensure that I didn't go quietly mad at home. Besides, I'd nearly finished all the books I'd got and they were not a cheap commodity to replenish.

Juliette chatted pleasantly while she cut. It was more small talk, of course, but quite bearable. I was getting used to what I had to say and, as I learnt more about Stephen's work, I had more to discuss about nutrition and healthcare. At long last I was also putting together a mental map of Lusaka. When districts or landmarks were mentioned I had some idea as to where they were.

Of course, I should not have worried about the haircut at all: the mop was cropped beautifully. I came back through to reception, receiving a fleeting look from my waiting husband, who quickly returned to the magazine I'd been reading earlier. I duly paid and then looked over Stephen's shoulder at the article. There was a photo of a rather entranced lady draped over the kitchen counter. He glanced up at me and smiled sheepishly.

"Ready to go?"

"Yes," I said, as he closed the magazine, replaced it on the rack and then escorted me from the salon.

"'Seven places to have an orgasm around the house'," he muttered. "Tell me, why don't we have a washing machine?"

A CHAT OVER COFFEE

It was September. Our mulberry tree was laden with dark green leaves and dropping juicy fruit all over what we generously termed 'the lawn'. The days were long and hot, and the ground was bone dry. Other trees were in full bloom: avenues of lilac jacaranda throughout the city, and flame trees with their delicious spray of red.

I could hardly believe we'd been in Zambia for three months. Three months! Marking it off in my mind, this was a quarter of the way through the first year and to my first flight home. The family all appeared quite content. Stephen was engrossed in his work and if I ignored all the grumbles about local timekeeping it seemed to be going quite well. We'd coined the phrase 'ZamTime' for the flexibility of keeping to deadlines. Matthew was having a great time in pre-school, not showing the slightest concern about leaving his mother and running off to play. Eleanor was showing a similar disregard for maternal love and concern, being increasingly uninterested in breast milk. All my efforts to ensure that this – the most hygienic way to give my daughter the milk she required – was possible while we lived in Africa and at eleven months old she was simply not bothered by it. It was the end of an era for me, though I was determined to see the month out.

So much was sorted, but I was conscious that, as a family, we hadn't yet settled upon a church to attend regularly. There were, of course, many things around the house that I would have liked to improve upon or speed up, but our church experience was beginning to feel hopeless. Africans had an inordinate amount of patience – or certainly their children did, sitting quietly through services lasting up to three hours. So far the only option for us had been for one of us to endure the service, the other to play outside with the children. Not a satisfactory, long-term solution.

But I had a smart new haircut, and I was taking it out for a cup of tea and a chocolate croissant at the bakery. Sherry was minding Eleanor so, childfree, I felt light-hearted and upbeat as I walked towards the shops. On entering I saw Rachel quietly enjoying a cup of coffee by herself and stopped to say hello. I don't know what peaceful time she was anticipating, but her open warmth meant that I quickly found myself sat down at her table and interrogating her about life in Zambia.

"How are you settling in?" she asked.

"Oh, fine! I'm hoping that within a couple of weeks we'll have a sofa and chair, which will be a huge relief. I chose the material on Monday and took it straight round. She said – and I quote – 'it will be ready in a week'."

She laughed. "So, they'll be ready in about a month, maybe longer?" There was an element of truth in this: I didn't expect anything to be completed within the original quoted time frame. ZamTime at its finest. But as I expected delays, I could be pleasantly surprised. The alternative bred frustration.

"Anyway, apart from a lack of furniture and everything being very basic, we are doing just fine." I was in a positive mood, buoyed by the delightful weather.

"Have you got your pictures up?"

For a moment I wondered what she was talking about, then I remembered that we had spoken after I purchased the wall hangings at the craft fair.

"They went up quickly – or, at least, they would have done but there is nothing quick about tapping a nail into the walls in our house. The concrete plaster must have been mixed with granite and steel. It is that hard to get anything into it."

"Amazing those termites can still get through. There is an entire wall at school which they've managed to eat through behind the plaster."

We chatted for a little while about the school. Her eldest was in reception and she saw no need to send her youngest for at least another year. I already held Rachel's parenting skills in such high regard that I was struck by parental guilt. I was sending Matthew five days a week (clearly I was a bad mother) but I knew that he loved it and that I would just be on edge with him doing all that painting and water-play at home. Rachel, in my view, was one of those 'super mums' for whom the mess and the chaos is part of the reason for having children.

The waitress came and took my order while Rachel explained that she was in the country permanently, having met and married her Zambian husband when teaching at a school in the north eight years ago.

"Are you enjoying Zambia?" she asked.

"It's OK," I said cagily, adding after a bit of thought, "It's not the UK."

"I know," she replied cheerily. She pointed at the blue sky and with the sweep of her hand gestured to the open space and fresh air. "Who'd want the UK when you've got this sun all the time?"

I smiled non-committally and looked down at my plate. She didn't know how little I wanted to move here, giving up my house, my friends and all that I understood. Yet even as I played with the flakes of croissant on my plate I wondered how much I still resented being here. Today was a positive day: I was determined to see the good in things, not the bad.

I moved the conversation on to talk about Stephen's work. He got so irate that all locals ate was nshima. Like eating potatoes all the time it hardly provided any nutritional value but, since it swells up inside the stomach, it made everyone feel satiated.

"Why can't they grow other crops?" I wondered. "Surely in this climate all sorts of vegetables and other sources of vitamins could be grown?"

"Well, it's not as hospitable as one would think," she ventured.

"I know: I have a very simplistic view of farming. But all the big farmers concentrate on growing maize, knowing that is the principal food, and so there is no alternative available to the rest of the population."

"My husband grows maize," she said. *Oh crikey*, I thought. I had probably just insulted her husband's farming abilities and I had to back-pedal rapidly.

"It's not any individual farmer's fault," I babbled. "It's a fault of the system. Everyone is encouraged to grow maize, they are promised good prices for it, and therefore it is widely grown. To diversify into other crops is risky, so why bother?"

In the shade of the mulberry tree

I could feel the colour rising in my cheeks and needed to change the subject quickly, as I might just dig myself a bigger and bigger hole. This poor woman hardly knew me and I was going off on a big rant against Zambian farming policy, about which I knew very little – a dangerous place from which to start an argument. I decided to ask about churches. At least it would sidetrack the conversation.

"I noticed on a table in your house last week that there was a children's book about Joseph and his coat of many colours. Do you go to church here?"

Rachel was evidently surprised by the question, coming out of the blue as it did, but soon recovered herself and responded.

"Yes, we go to a small house church over in Makeni."

"What is it like? Is it good?"

"Erm, yes. We enjoy it." She sipped her coffee before elaborating. "It started from a group of families that did an Alpha course together, and wanted to build a church that would cater for the children."

"Ah – yes. That is where we have a problem. We have tried a different church each week since being here, and none seem very child-friendly – at least, not for *our* children."

And I recounted to her our various experiences so far. I spoke of the church with the clicking vicar, who came into church in his robes, leading the singing and making rhythmic clicking noises as he did so. He was the only one so far to have mentioned HIV/AIDS, which gave him bonus points in our book. We tried the Anglican Cathedral, with its beautiful stained glass windows that reminded me of the Piper window at Coventry Cathedral. At another church we'd been welcomed with gifts of roses, then made to stand in a line outside the building afterwards in the burning

A chat over coffee

midday sun to be greeted by all the attendees – probably two hundred of them. We had sat on pews in a central church established by Victorian missionaries over a century ago; and in another sat on plastic chairs, numbered boldly to provide accountability, while our children crawled around on the dusty concrete floor and through holes that would, one day, become doorways. We had endured long services with locals still drifting in towards the end, and we had listened to sermons that were simultaneously being translated into Nyanja, thus doubling their already generous length.

"Last Sunday I tried the Miracle Life Church again," I recounted to Rachel. "Given it has a Sunday school I thought it was worth giving it a second chance, although the first time we were rather put off because there were two lengthy sermons: one before the collection and then the real one later. It has a lot going for it, with lively gospel music and there is a definite sense of worship. Last week I had to go out and walk around the car park with Matthew during the sermon, but they had loudspeakers set up outside so I could hear what was being said. The minister astounded me. He was just back from visiting the US. One place he'd been to was just setting up a Bible school – no doubt a worthy institution – so he had decided to donate $1000 of his own money and had pledged that his church in Lusaka would match that gift. One thousand dollars! From a congregation that, for the large part, struggle to earn that in a year! How dare he pledge that money to the US, such a rich and wealthy economy?"

Rachel turned her spoon idly in her coffee. I had the sense that she'd heard it all before.

"There is a lot of prosperity teaching in Zambia," she said. "You know – many think that if they believe in God, He will provide you with riches and that wealth is actually an indicator of how faithful you are, or have been. It's hard to eradicate, given how appealing it is to the poor."

"Yes, I can see that. His sermon did have that leaning as well, perhaps not so blatantly but definitely there. Combining that with another half-hour sermon on what we should do with money immediately preceding the collection, I think we shall be giving the whole thing a miss."

"Well, you are welcome to come to our church. We meet at nine o'clock." I raised an eyebrow. "Yes, I know, it is early, but some of them go on to polo matches so it has to be that time. You go down the Kafue road, then…"

I listened blankly. I had not a clue where any of the landmarks she was describing were. Rachel spotted my incomprehension. "I tell you what: be at your gate at 8.30 am and follow us."

✧

The sermon was given by a South African man in shorts. I suspect that sort of thing is outlawed in the UK, and not just because of the weather, but it suited us fine. Everyone sat in the living room of a church member's house, furniture pushed to one side and chairs lined up with an aisle down the middle. It was the first time I had sat through a church service sitting on a sofa. A small group led the singing from the front, interspersed with a short story and prayers, after which the children (who easily made up half the congregation) left. Taking Matthew with them through to the kitchen and bedroom I discovered that Rachel led the Sunday school, teaching the children simple songs and Bible stories. Not one child was fractious or out of sorts and Matthew was totally absorbed.

A chat over coffee

Afterwards we stayed for coffee on the veranda, together with a wide assortment of homemade cakes and biscuits representing the many nationalities that had attended the service. I knew I shouldn't judge a church based on food, but it really helped. The children ran around the garden, some of the older ones playing cricket, the younger ones on climbing frames or peering at the rabbit in his hutch.

Gazing out across the garden, watching the children play, I quietly acknowledged that I had found a spiritual home; that here, with this small group of Christian families, I was confident that I could grow in faith and find true friendship.

FORTUNE

I was sitting outside in the shade of a frangipani tree with a group of mothers, caught up in conversation about sleepless nights and baby food recipes, when I got the SMS. In all honesty I was finding my weekly regimen of travels from one baby group to another increasingly tedious. Everyone was lovely, but the routine had little else to stretch my brain cells.

The message read: PLS CUM 2 OFFICE @14 2 START WORK.

After deciphering the text I stared at my phone in amazement. Months of waiting, being uncertain as to whether I would get firstly a job and secondly a work permit, and suddenly I was to start work just like that. I gazed round at the other mothers: relaxed, chatting, enjoying the luxuries of being an expat spouse – and went into mild panic. Did I really want to do this?

Shouldn't I stay at home, bring up the children, be the perfect domestic wife and mother?

Then I remembered Sherry, lovingly playing with Eleanor on her knee; or Precious throwing and catching balls with Matthew – both women of unerring patience. And I knew they would be in safe hands, and safer if I was also happy.

∽

I sat in the office surrounded by paperwork, reports for overseas donors and requests for money. There was a cool breeze wafting through the windows, the floral patterned curtains shielding the worst of the sun and fluttering in the wind. I moved a heavy book to act as a paperweight before the drafts of the report I was working on flew across the room. The accounts office was one of the coolest in the building, only catching the sun late afternoon but still it was hot. Taking a swig from my water bottle I wondered just when it was going to rain. I'd been in Zambia for four months and nothing – not a drop.

The school children were running around outside, the tinkling sound of their excitement drifting in as they played in the dusty space. There were a couple of rusting swings and climbing frames and virtually no shelter from the sun, but the children were having fun, loving their freedom from class like every other child in the world.

A child's screams broke my reverie and I glanced out of the window. It really was incomprehensible that I was there. I'd resolved never to touch accountancy in the developing world: who in their right mind would attempt this in an environment of corruption and greed? Corruption was endemic to the country, cheating the system from top to toe. Sometimes it was blatant, payments in brown envelopes; sometimes it was subtle, for example I could not understand the need for 'sitting allowances', extra non-taxable payments for people who attended meetings, even if the meetings were part of and inextricable from one's full-time (paid) work. Sometimes it was overlooked simply because of the poverty of the recipient. For instance, you might pay a little extra to a security guard who had watched your car knowing that his take-home wages would barely cover the cost of his travel, let alone rent and food.

Yet here I was, taking a position as financial controller, leading an accounts department in a local, charitably-based organisation. Zambia seemed to be doing strange things to me, taking me far from my comfort zone.

I blamed Richie entirely. Sure, I mentioned that I was an accountant. And yes, I did say I was bored… repeatedly. And I did express an interest in working for an organisation that was doing so much good for the people of Zambia. But did he have to take me literally? Just because he knew that the accountant at EFZ was leaving, did he have to suggest me? How life's plots twist and turn. I felt I was in the right place now, using my accountancy to serve people who had so little. Perhaps in my own small way I would make a difference.

Not that it had been an easy ride so far. I looked at my work colleagues in accounts, Maggie and Winnie. They were so tolerant of my blunderings, my cultural *faux pas*, my errors of judgement. Maggie was busy completing the cashbook with the day's cheques. This was done in pen, longhand, across the wide, ruled accounting books. Each project or department had its own column and, as more and more was taken on by the organisation, the book did not appear to be wide enough. The system worked, but was not totally satisfactory. I noted on my to-do list that I should chase the quotes and options for computerising the process.

Maggie's knowledge of the organisation was immense, partly from years of experience and partly from her innate intelligence. In her spare time she was studying for her professional accountancy exams and she had just come back from maternity leave after her fourth child, taking the mere three months that the government allowed. Remembering how exhausting the first few months were I marvelled at her bright presence. She must have been longing to be with her baby, although with four children at home I wondered whether she enjoyed the peace our office brought.

My attention turned to Winnie, working hard to balance the petty cash. Since instigating a rule that petty cash was only available at certain times of the day her job had become a lot easier. Although it hadn't entirely eliminated the requests for money at odd times, it had certainly kept them under control and limited them to emergencies. I smiled at her studiousness. I had only discovered the day before that she actually held an accounts qualification, much to my chagrin. She was not a natural accountant like Maggie, but I was blessed to be working with two such diligent and honest women.

"Ba Fortune!" I heard from the corridor. Joan was calling for him. I heard his voice in response. Rev Fortune Mwiza was Head of the Church department, responsible for the support of preachers and churches throughout the country as well as the library and bookshop on-site, and was the pastor who was horrified to find condoms in his office. In his spare time he was the minister for a growing church in Kalingalinga, seeking funding for church buildings to house the five-hundred-strong congregation. He came up the corridor, knocked and entered.

In the shade of the mulberry tree

"Ah, Madam Catharine, muli bwanji!"

"Bwino bwanji"

"Bwino!" It was a test, a daily test of my Nyanja. Thankfully, it rarely got further than this greeting.

"How can I help you?" I asked.

"Ah, yes. I am sorry, but I need some money."

I raised my eyebrows.

"Yes, yes, I know. It is late for this morning, but I have to go into town and there is no vehicle."

"None at all?"

"No. Joan tells me she needs the Toyota for project work and that she has arranged a meeting at the UN. Please, can I have thirty pin for taxis?"

I took a deep breath. *Why can they never plan ahead properly, or communicate with one another until it is too late?* The vehicle was bought with project money for project work, so Joan, as head of that department, did get first call.

"Please? I have to get this advert in the paper for the David Wilkerson conference and it must be in before 15 hours to meet the deadlines. See!" He waved a previous request slip at me. "See – I have the cheque for the advert. Just now I don't have the transport to get it there."

He smiled at me, pleading with his eyes. I released my breath. "Oh, go on," I smiled. "Winnie, can you organise thirty thousand for Fortune?"

"Of course."

"Oh, thank you, thank you," said Fortune. I was both smiling and shaking my head as he took the money and rushed off on his errand, calling for the driver as he went.

ಎఎ

Twice a week the bookshop was encircled with plastic chairs as the workers who were in the office had devotions before work. On this occasion Joan was leading. She was in charge of relief and development work and recently back from maternity leave, a cheerful woman who worked extraordinarily hard to keep all the projects running smoothly from the distance of head office. In addition to her full-time job at EFZ she ran a dressmaker's business from home and was looking to record an album. Her beautiful voice rang out, clear and strong. It was undeniably African, but without any of the nasal whine that can accompany their higher pitched tones. Of course, the Africans are known for their wonderful singing: how else would we have all the negro spirituals that have been integrated into our Western culture? Everyone else in the room joined in, harmonies natural, fluent, falling into place as if they had been written by the greatest composer, yet all from the heart, from an innate musicality that enabled the tunes to rise and fall, to grow and contract, to sing of God's love. When they sang in their local tongues I could not join in, but caught the occasional 'Jesu' or 'Hallelujah' and shared their praise.

Fortune said a few words, expanding on the psalm he was planning as a Bible reading for Sunday's service. No doubt this was a practice run for the sermon. He often did this and, although it sometimes felt a bit of a cheat (why not something new and fresh for this occasion?) I told myself off for such uncharitable thoughts: he ran an entire church in the few hours left of his week after EFZ's work was done.

He suddenly turned to me and asked, "Catharine, what do you think?"

What did I think?

I thought I was in the right place at the right time. I was supposed to be here, among these local people who were working so hard for their brothers and sisters in other parts of the country. Their commitment and love was a daily revelation.

I thought I was doing all right as a mother by returning to work. It was only part-time, so I still got my Friday mornings at the bakery (with tea and croissants and my daughter's face covered in chocolate). I thought I'd never fully escape the guilt of working, nor the guilt of not working.

I thought I was brave to have stopped the anti-malarials for the family, especially as the rainy season approached. I had worked out they were the cause of Matthew's nightmares, having recognised the bad dreams always came two or three nights after taking his weekly tablet. Yet stopping the drugs that prevented malaria? What madness was that!

I thought being here, in Zambia, had made my husband very happy.

And I thought I was too. Africa was weaving its magic spell, seeping in through my pores, penetrating the layers of skin and bone and touching on my heart. When did I last weep for home? When did I seriously miss the UK such that I pined to go back? I couldn't remember. I was looking forward to my father coming to visit in December, but realised that I'd not actually spoken to him for weeks.

I might not be where I thought I would be at this point in my life, but it was hardly a bad place. My move had, to my surprise, been to a freedom and contentment that I'd never envisaged. I was doing a job I enjoyed, I had new friends all around me and a life of comparative luxury.

What did I think?

Fortune coughed, expectantly.

I thought I should have been concentrating more on his homily in the first place.

CREEPY CRAWLY CREATURES

It was an ordinary evening. Children asleep, Stephen and I were sitting quietly in the house reading books when we heard an unusual noise. I looked up. "What was that?" I asked. There was another pinging sound on the roof, then another.

"Rain!" we screamed in unison.

We ran outside, delighted to see these few friendly drops fall on the parched land. We skipped about on the scrub of lawn, dancing joyfully as the beads of water tickled our faces.

A minute later it was all over, but hope flooded our minds: this year there would be rain. This year the crops would be watered. This year there would be food for all.

The next day the old pattern resumed. It started bright and sunny, gradually clouding over after lunch until by evening it looked ominous. The heat was stifling, perhaps even stickier since our brief brush with rainfall. Yet there remained hope.

※

It was half-term and I had more time with Matthew so, for a treat, I took him on a trip to the airport. We could stand outside on the viewing deck and watch all the comings and goings. There were aeroplanes taxiing close by: the smaller ones filling up with tourists who were flying out to the national parks; the big South African Airways plane being filled with luggage. Matthew delighted in the chance to see tractors towing the mobile steps for the aircraft and moving trailers full of luggage. We had timed our visit well, for despite being the country's main international airport, it was by no means the busiest airport in the world. I'd heard rumours about low-cost airlines being interested in setting it up as a hub for the region. Zambia is landlocked but shares borders with eight other countries and there was plenty of room at the airport for expansion. It could easily have taken more international flights and, with the downfall of Zimbabwean foreign relations, could have been an excellent place for connecting flights to regional capitals. Even as it was, with planes of all sizes taking off and landing, it provided an hour of high entertainment for Matthew.

On our way home I called in to see Daniel. I had some new designs for him: a large shelving unit into which I planned to put some baskets woven by the woman behind the Coca Cola trailer at Longacres. This was becoming a necessity for us as the children's toys were strewn everywhere and I needed storage to hide them away.

Creepy crawly creactures

Our need, though, was nothing compared to Daniel's. Mutende got halfway through her chemotherapy course the previous week when it transpired that the hospital had no more of the drugs. Daniel was told there might be some in Zimbabwe, and so now he planned to travel. What sort of healthcare was it when a child was started on chemotherapy, the only option available to save her life, but no consideration was given to whether the hospital had, or could order in, the required drugs? It was the main teaching tertiary care hospital for the whole country, which one might expect to have a reasonable stock and purchasing policy so that no patient had to do without.

Not only were the drugs expensive but so too was the travel to obtain them. We had decided to help by ordering some more custom-designed furniture.

As usual Daniel greeted us with a broad smile.

"Muli bwanji!"

Matthew piped up, "Hello!" and then busied himself with chasing the chickens around the yard. Nobody seemed too bothered by this (although the hens were a little flustered) so I spent a few minutes explaining my design to Daniel. He nodded in understanding, asking a few questions about my measurements and confirming that the shelves should be two centimetres thick. While he calculated the cost, I called to Matthew, who was now a little over-excited and frustrated at being outwitted by the poultry. I persuaded him to start counting small off-cuts of wood instead.

Daniel returned with a price. He was most apologetic for it, but we required two very long lengths of hardwood, and that would be difficult to find. It would not come cheap. I considered his price and translated it into sterling. The piece would cost little more than a flat pack back home, yet I was getting mukwa, a beautiful solid hardwood, cut to my own specific measurements so that it would fit perfectly into our living room. I wondered how on earth Daniel could afford to make it and have enough left over to fund Mutende's healthcare. I left a substantial deposit, hoping that it would pay for the Harare trip, scooped Matthew up and returned home.

In all reality, I wondered how Mutende was going to survive. Stephen and I had been to see her just a couple of weeks before. She looked shockingly worse than her desperate 'white tongue' state three months earlier. Weakened by the chemotherapy she lay inert in her hospital cot. Her hair had fallen out in patches and although her eyes were less swollen there was no mistaking the deathly sickness.

She was in a small room, packed with beds but which had the bountiful privilege of only one child per mattress. It seemed a marked improvement on the malnutrition wards in the next block. Cynicism abounded: donors generally seemed to be happy to fund children's cancer care, but there wasn't the same glamour for medical intervention into malnutrition. Perhaps this was because cancer is an isolated illness. Curing malnutrition requires drastic changes to home life, income, food security, national farming policy and much more besides.

Colourful cotton curtains caught the breeze, but this could not hide the ingrained smell of illness, of vomit and incontinence overlain by chlorine. Stephen had often commented that the hospital suffered from lack of water and electricity, disrupting his research or computer data entry. Rumour alleged that the hospital had not paid its electricity bill, hence the frequent blackouts. And, since the water was pumped from boreholes across the hospital, no electricity meant no water. Generous donors offered to build more water pumps, but paying for the ongoing power and upkeep of the existing ones might have been more useful. For now, the water supply was limited to two hours a day: barely enough to keep the place hygienic.

How was Daniel's family going to survive this? It was expensive to get daily buses to and from the hospital to visit their daughter, and there was little chance of her moving anywhere else in her current state. UTH did not provide food, so someone had to come on a daily basis to ensure Mutende's basic needs were met. The issue with the lack of drugs and the requirement to travel to Zimbabwe to buy them added insult to injury. Even with the right medicine Mutende's chances were poor. But what choice did Daniel have? To give up on his seven-year-old daughter?

I glanced at Matthew in the rear-view mirror, engrossed in his plastic toy aeroplane. I knew I couldn't give up on him: I would fight to the end, spend every penny I had to ensure he had the best healthcare possible, the most up-to-date treatment. Why should Daniel be any different?

∽

Ever since 'Happy-birthday-Daddy' was planted beneath the bedroom window Stephen had been on a mission to improve the back of the plot. Evans, the communal gardener, had been recruited to spend his afternoon allotted to our garden in planting grass in the orange dust, taking cuttings from elsewhere on the complex. As I watched the rows go in I feared they were a little too far apart to develop into a luscious green carpet.

Of course, planting into dust required a lot of watering, so Stephen had also invested in a sprinkler system to go around the garden beds. It was somewhat temperamental but to date the majority of the tough grass was surviving. Stephen justified all this planting as "reducing the amount of dust in the house." Judging by the amount Sherry brushed up and out every morning it was having minimal effect so far.

The advent of rain had encouraged Stephen to extend his plans for the garden and, given his farming background, Richie had been called in as agricultural adviser.

"But I'm a dairy farmer," he protested. No matter: he knew more than either of us.

Stephen was concerned about the yellowing of the grass ("No rain," said Richie) and the unevenness of the lawn ("Previous rains," said Richie). After some protracted discussions Stephen decided to invest in black soil to fertilise the lawn. We all had resulting responsibilities. Evans had spent a week away from lawn production at the back and instead had aerated the ground under the washing line. Richie had been charged with purchasing the black soil. And I was to keep Precious from hanging out washing on the days that soil arrived.

Sherry greeted me on the driveway as I returned from Daniel's. Eleanor was grinning over her shoulder, cocooned in the chitenge slung across Sherry's back. I smiled broadly at my baby daughter and helped Matthew out of The Bishop before taking her for a big cuddle.

At this point Richie pulled up behind me with another load of black soil. Glancing at the washing line I saw that everyone except me had been successful at their allotted garden tasks. Sherry hurried off inside to call Precious.

As he delivered this final load Richie laughed at the peculiarities of Zambian economics. "The first bag cost me K20,000," he said. "I may be their only business, as I'm not sure who stops along Kamloops to trade, when

Creepy crawly creactures

there is such choice in Kalingalinga. So how does this work: one bag, twenty pin; four bags for ten pin." He scratched his head in bemusement. "I'll never understand this country!"

All my accountancy training could not explain this away.

Evans appeared to shovel the soil out of the back of the pick-up. I knew Stephen would spend the early evening gently raking it out over the small plot: about ten square metres beneath the washing line were benefiting from our gardening expertise. At least the clothes will grow well, I thought to myself.

Back on the front drive, Richie was teaching Matthew how to bat.

"Are you left- or right-handed?" he asked.

Matthew looked up at his god: he hadn't a clue which was which. He grabbed the bat and ran.

"Yes, well, that is the basic principle," said Richie, and took off after him. They darted around until finally Matthew was caught. Eleanor, firmly wedged on my hip, clapped her hands in delight.

"Come! Come!" Evans was beckoning to us. "Ssh!" he added, creeping mysteriously down the road.

We wondered what on earth he had seen, but all was made clear when he gently pulled aside a branch of a bush. Below, hidden in the leaves, was a chameleon.

It was a most distinctive creature, scaly looking with a hunched back. The tail curled in a spiral and his eyes bulged out of their sockets, watching us warily. He didn't move. Only visible was the rise and fall of rapid breathing. Whispering, I told Matthew that chameleons change colour.

"But he's just green," he said.

"Yes, I know he is just now, but he would change colour to suit where he is, to blend in with the background. Why do you think he is green right now? What else is green?"

Matthew pulled a frown as he thought hard. "The leaves."

"Well done! Yes, he's green because of the leaves."

Evans was smiling at this conversation and took hold of the creature, putting him on the tarmac.

"He's still green, Mummy!"

"Wait, wait – be patient."

Patience, of course, was not a two-year-old's strength. I made conversation to keep Matthew interested, but was surprised by how green the chameleon remained. Evans put him back on the branch and then, only then, did I see that his previous green camouflage, which had been so good that I was astonished Evans had ever noticed him, was now poor. His time on the road had made an impact on him, turning the whole vibrant green a shade or two greyer. We left the chameleon in peace and walked home.

∽

Despite that first sprinkling, this year the rains were late. Fortune assured me that under Kenneth Kaunda the first rains of the season came on October 24th, Independence Day, every year: I had no evidence to either prove or disprove the assertion, although maintained a healthy dose of scepticism. By mid-November the rains were clearly established. We had several heavy downpours and the humidity was becoming unbearable. My two-litre bottle of water at work each day was barely enough to get me through. The occasional rainfalls provided brief respite from the searing heat. Rain was immediately followed by scorching sun which vaporised the puddles, so that within an hour you wouldn't know that rain had fallen.

In turn this increased the humidity, so the next shower was even more longed-for.

Rain had brought more new creatures into our lives. Firstly, there was a boom in the number of chongololos around the property. These were large, blackish-brown millipedes which curl up into coils, looking for all the world like ammonite fossils. To Matthew they were fascinating. Eleanor merely crawled up to investigate them as an alternative snack.

One evening just before she left for the day, Precious called me through to the front door. She pointed to the ground, not half a metre from the entrance. "Snake," she said.

I looked at it in horror. A small, black slithery creature not more than six inches long was laid out in front of me. It looked more like a worm than a snake until I saw it move: the slithering twists confirmed its identity. I was panicked into immobility, staring pointlessly at the creature. Eleanor crawling up rapidly from behind shook me out of my stupor. I grabbed hold of her before she fell off the step and onto the snake or, worse, tried to eat it.

"You must shut your doors at 18 hours," warned Precious. For once I was in no mood to argue. Deftly she moved the creature, before calling Evans to dispose of it completely. I drew the children back inside and firmly closed the door.

Overnight the clouds burst open and raindrops hammered the tin roofs. I lay in bed listening to the rain. It was extraordinarily cosy, cocooned by the sheets, the mosquito net and a solid concrete house. Nothing else could be heard: no cicadas, no birds, no frogs. For now we were escaping rain in daylight hours but Sherry informed me that by January I should anticipate a monsoon-like downpour every day that would drench everything in sight. "February, rain," she explained.

"But by April, no rain. May, no rain. June, no rain. No rain until October." Ah yes – Independence Day and its ritual expectation of autumnal rain. But of course, I realised, it wasn't autumn here. It was, if anything, spring, or perhaps the height of summer as the heat was at its most intense. My muddled up southern/northern hemisphere seasons confused my understanding of the annual cycle.

In the morning I woke to sunshine, and a porch coated with leaves. On closer inspection, I discovered they were wings. In amongst them were some orange cocoons, no more than a couple of centimetres long. Stepping out, there was an uncomfortable crunch beneath my feet. Sherry arrived, absolutely on time, as always.

"Ah! Inswa!" she exclaimed. I looked at her, hoping for more. "Inswa. Flies. See, the body." The small bodies had been discarded along with the wings. It turned out our porch had become an inswa graveyard. "They like the light," she explained, pointing upwards. Leaving an outside light on at night had its disadvantages and I felt responsible for the death of hundreds of innocent flies.

Later friends told me they were a type of termite. The larger ones were a delicacy – fried in a little oil with salt sprinkled over, a little chopped onion if you like – although I never had the courage to try. Sherry spent two or three mornings sweeping up the gossamer wings.

Then, as soon as they had come, they were gone.

THE DAY NO-ONE REMEMBERED

I woke with a start, some unknown event disrupting sleep. In the quiet of dawn I listened out: no sound from the children, so I relaxed and reached for the alarm clock. Five-twenty am. What a peculiar time to have roused. In the distance I heard people beginning their days, the crowing of the local cockerels and singing from the apostolic church. A cat (or was it a rat?) ran across the roof – perhaps he was the cause of my early day.

I slumped back onto the pillow, staring up at the mosquito net. Friday. At long last it was the end of the week. Once again it had been hectic, filled with trips across town to pre-school and juggling work demands around the family's schedule. Friday was my day off and I could look forward to a morning with my daughter at the café.

In the shade of the mulberry tree

Then I remembered what day it was. 21st November. Sixteen years this year. Sixteen years since I was sixteen, since…

I shut my eyes to block the memories that I knew would come, that I wanted to come, that I dreaded coming. I opened them again and sat up. No point staying in bed now, there was no chance of drifting back into sleep, not even for that blissful half hour before the alarm went off.

I slipped out of bed and went through to the kitchen, glancing at the thermometer on my way past. Already twenty-one degrees: it was going to be another hot and humid day. The sporadic showers had only increased our desperation for the proper rains to come. The heat was draining, exhausting. As I padded across the concrete floor I was grateful for the cold touch on my feet, knowing that by two o'clock I would be lying on the floor to absorb the cool it provided. Finally I was grateful for the shade of the mulberry tree.

I filled the kettle from the water filter, put it on and stared out of the kitchen window at the small courtyard beyond. The maids had put a couple of the garden chairs out and sat there in the middle of the morning to have their breakfast, or lunch – I was never quite sure which it was. Already the tropical sun was shining down on our feeble attempts to grow plants in a couple of pots, their chances of survival diminishing with every minute, every ray of sun burning up their leaves.

The kettle boiled. As I poured water over a teabag, I reflected how precious a commodity it was here. My work colleagues had been praying for weeks that the rains would come, the memories of the drought two years earlier still fresh in their minds. They continued to feed the families that had lost their crops, their livelihood, their homes during that season. Mum would have been pleased to see the work being done here.

The day no-one remembered

She'd always supported Christian Aid. And Samaritans. And the church. And Cancer Research.

I cradled my mug and looked heavenwards. Today. Why today? I took my drink through to the living room and sank into the sofa. The view changed to the shady garden, much gloomier as the sun struggled to reach through the leaves of the mulberry tree and touch the ground below. It matched my mood. Why me? I sighed, knowing there was no answer, that I couldn't change anything. Sixteen years: half my life. It was improbable that anyone else would recognise the significance of this. My husband probably wouldn't even remember what day it was.

As if on cue I heard the alarm go off in the next room. One...two...three... Come on, switch it off! Seven...eight...a bump, a groan, some fumbling... twelve...thirt- At last! Success! Then silence. Oh heck, I thought, no World Service blasting through the wall. He's gone back to sleep again. He won't be wondering where I am then, won't be worrying about his sleepless wife. How come he can fall asleep again? Can't he just this once have some sensitivity?

The irrationality of my anger finally spilt through into tears. It was just not fair. My family were so far away, not that any of them would necessarily recognise this landmark, another statistic to record and pass by. I rang my sister when she had lived as much time without Mum as with her: I was unlikely even to speak to her or Dad today. No-one else was likely to remember, not even my husband. Why should he? He never knew her, he wasn't there. I was on my own. On my own, thousands of miles from home, with no-one I could share this with, no-one who would understand.

My friend's mum had told me that I would always be someone whose mother died when she was sixteen. Her mother, too, had died when she was a child. As the years had gone by I'd come to recognise the truth in what she'd said. I had gone through my entire adult life as a half-orphan. Most people wouldn't know that Mum had died; when I spoke only about Dad they assumed my parents were divorced, probably badly.

How do you answer a question such as, "Where do your parents live?" when you only have one? The first and quickest option was: "York." This avoided any awkwardness, but was technically untrue. Only one parent lived in York. My mother's burnt remains were in a graveyard, marked by a stone that was gradually being overgrown by grass since none of us lived near enough to tend it regularly. My preferred response was: "My Dad lives in York." This gently corrected the error but generally left the questioner confused as to what happened with the other fifty per cent of my parents. In bolshy moods, when I wished to shock the listener, the third option was chosen: "My Dad lives in York. My mother died when I was sixteen. She had cancer – breast cancer – although she eventually died of cancer of the bone, or perhaps of the chemotherapy, or the build-up of gunk on her lungs. I actually don't know as I never saw the death certificate."

Tears were rolling down my cheeks. I pictured her in hospital the last time I saw her, hooked up to a tube that drained her lungs into a large bell-jar below the bed. She was so frail, having just received her second dose of chemo. I was trying to discreetly see if her hair was falling out, but really she still looked very much like Mum – tired, weak, quiet, but definitely Mum. She did smile, even then. I told her I wasn't sure how I could cope with Dad – he was being a sixteen-year-old girl's nightmare, over-protective, over-loving. She smiled sadly. She couldn't do anything, not then, not anymore.

It's funny, the things you remember. I was wearing my yellow jumper over my school uniform, something I

The day no-one remembered

foolishly thought fashionable. A few weeks later I put it in a hot wash and it shrank, never to be worn again.

We didn't know then just how close to death she was. It turned out to be a very bad week, as the next day we had to have our eleven-year-old dog put down. She had a growth in her stomach and that was the kindest thing to do. Dad and I struggled so hard to tell Gran on the phone, both of us in floods of tears. Where was my sister then? So often she speaks of being left out by Dad and me at that time. In the cool of the sitting room, far from home, I wept in sorrow that she carries that as rejection to this day.

It happened again when Dad told us on the Friday, following a meeting with the nurses, that Mum was not going to survive, that she had weeks, probably only days, to live. I ran to hug Dad; my sister came and hugged us both. Why didn't I put my arms around her as well? Why is grief so irrational, so insensitive to others?

It was the following morning that she died.

Sixteen years ago. I glanced up at the clock and corrected for the time-difference – almost sixteen years to the minute. It never goes away, the memory, the knowledge, the gaping hole in your life. I still felt unfairly done by. Nobody to do my washing for me when I go home, no food parcels sent out, no being filled in on the gossip from the other mums in the village. And now – here, so horribly alone.

I sobbed uncontrollably into the cushions on the sofa.

I'll never know why me, will I? It is my cross to bear, my burden to care for, my trauma to live with. She's never known my husband, she'll never meet her grandchildren. She didn't see me get my degree, meet my first boyfriend, get highlights in my hair, walk down

In the shade of the mulberry tree

the aisle. She's missed so much, and I've missed so much more.

She was a beautiful woman. Not traditionally stunning, but she had a beauty in her heart that shone through into every aspect of her life. She was loved by so many but I had the privilege of calling her Mum. I sat up, giving the cushion a final punch. No-one could take that from me.

Slowly I pulled myself together, wiped the remaining tears. Calm returned. I took a sip of my tea. Out of the window I saw a small, blue-breasted bird pecking at the dry soil under the tree. He's hopeful of a treat for breakfast, I mused, bringing a smile to my face. He'd be lucky: the earth was rock-hard and any sensible worms had buried themselves deep underground. I heard my baby daughter whimper and recognised the first signs of daily family life. My peace would soon be shattered. I downed the rest of my tea and returned the mug to the kitchen.

The whimper became a wail as she wanted to escape the confines of her cot. I needed to rescue Eleanor from her perceived grief. Grief? The irony. She was crying because she wanted me, she needed me, she felt left out and alone. I turned and walked back through the house. My husband would remember the following day: it's his father's birthday and he usually remembers then that he forgot the day before. And possibly Dad would call. Feelings might be unspoken but it didn't mean they weren't there.

I opened the door to the children's bedroom. Matthew was sitting up in bed surrounded by an assortment of toys, reading his books. So absorbed was he that he barely noticed my entrance. I reached to lift my daughter from the cot and greeted her with a kiss. The crying stopped. She smiled, sure of my mirrored response. It was my turn to be Mum.

BETTER THE DEVIL YOU KNOW

I was back in the office, another brilliantly sunny day. I was presented with a cash request slip. I read it through, before asking Maggie for help.

"What does this say?"

"Broom," she said, deciphering the hieroglyphics.

"Ah, yes! What's happened to the old one?"

"It is worn out."

"Do you know that for sure, or are you just assuming so."

She laughed. "No, it is finished."

"OK. And what about this? Why do we need so many candles? In fact, why do we need candles at all? We don't work at night and, as a general rule, we have electricity."

"They will be for the polish," she said, as if that explained everything.

In the shade of the mulberry tree

"Polish?"

"Yes, see – there is also the paraffin."

"I'd been going to come to that. Why are we buying paraffin?"

"For the polish."

"The polish?" I repeated.

"Yes, you mix it with the candles."

I stared at her disbelievingly. "Why not simply buy a tin of floor polish?"

"It is too expensive."

I looked at her, then the chitty, then asked, "Are you sure? These are for the polish?"

"Oh, yes." She clapped her hands, bobbed a curtsy and smiled.

I picked up my pen and signed off the request, while images of our cleaner slicing up candles and mashing them in bottles of paraffin floated around my head.

❧

Winnie and Maggie always laughed at me (in a very polite fashion) for bringing in two litres of water every day but the tap water was unsafe for my Western stomach. The heat was stifling and we were desperate for rain. Having finished my water, I nipped to the toilet. On the door was a sign telling me to clean up if I 'sprinkle as I tinkle'. I often wondered how much that applied to the ladies' lavatory.

Coming back into the office I informed Winnie that there was no toilet paper.

"It is kept at reception," she told me.

I went out to the entrance and asked the receptionist for a roll.

"Just a minute," she said. She left for the office of the Executive Director, returning with a key from his secretary. She unlocked the battered filing cabinet in the corner, pulled open the bottom drawer and extracted a roll of dusky pink paper from the package within. It was the cheapest version at the supermarket, the paper that reminded me of the early days of recycled paper, when the toilet roll manufacturers hadn't realised that just because we were eco-friendly it didn't mean we wanted to wipe our bottoms with sandpaper. While I thanked the receptionist, she reversed the rigmarole, locking the cabinet and returning the keys.

When I got back I asked Winnie why we kept the toilet paper at reception; or rather, why we kept it under lock and key in the filing cabinet there.

"Otherwise it will get stolen," she said.

∾

The Executive Director was away again, this time at a regional conference in South Africa. Since I started work I had barely seen him. It was frustrating as his signature was required on all the cheques, so we had to plan everything for the windows of time when he was present. Joan had just come in to see me, requesting some project money and letting off steam about his absence. She was voicing her frustrations about the system. She couldn't get the money she needed at the time required. I sympathised but my hands were tied.

Everything was run on a tight budget and I knew that the ED wanted to organise a trip to America to fundraise for the organisation. I wondered whether or not I would give him money. His role in the organisation was increasingly political: not siding with any one party but seeking a review of the country's constitution, being the public voice of the churches in Zambia. Would the Americans have wanted to give money to such a role? On the one hand I knew all the hard work that went on in the office, people who worked long hours for meagre pay. Yet so much got lost in the system as chiefs were placated, community leaders empowered. However, there was a great need for money to cover administrative costs: not just staff, but telephones and mobiles, computerising the offices, storage, security, paper and ink. The risks of theft meant there were controls over everything (not just the toilet paper), which led to more paperwork and staffing. Was it better to fund something, or nothing?

I tried to placate Joan and together we put together a plan for the project resources, making the best use of what we'd already got. I showed her the bank forms I'd signed to become a signatory on the accounts, hoping that would break some of the bottlenecks. We joked over the ED's face in the paper (really, he needed new glasses) and parted on good terms.

※

"Maggie, why are we paying transport costs for all the delegates?"

"They are coming to the training course."

"But they have chosen to do this. And the course is free."

"They have to get there."

"Yes, but…" I knew I wasn't going to win that argument so I tried a different tack. "Doesn't fifteen pin seem excessive? A bus fare is only about two or three thousand."

Maggie shrugged her shoulders. "It is what they get. Some will pay more, some less."

I sighed and gave up. It was what was expected. It was also within the project budget, as approved by the international donors. Reluctantly I signed the request and waited to see what sort of receipts the project manager could offer as evidence later.

It was payday. Nearly forty members of staff would be at the door before 15 hours expecting an envelope of cash.

Maggie had returned from the bank with their money – millions of kwacha hidden in the capacious black handbag used for bank trips. I offered to help, as I could see it would take the rest of the day to count out the thousands of kwacha notes. And we had it comparatively easy: a year earlier there weren't K20,000 or K50,000 notes. Maggie was twice my speed, rapidly flicking through piles of notes. Every note got counted: Maggie didn't trust the bank's counting machine or the bundled notes. We worked our way through the spreadsheet, making the best we could of our petty cash so that we got exact salaries. There were a few dips into our own purses, finding small change, ensuring that the lowest paid got the full amount first.

With two people left to go I realised we only had enough notes to pay one of them.

"What's happened?" I asked. "Didn't we get the exact amount from the bank?"

I double-checked the total on our spreadsheet against the cash cheque I had signed. Same amount, so it should have balanced. I sighed, realising I was going to have to double-check every envelope.

Maggie started on my small pile of finished pay slips.

"There is an extra K10,000 here," she said from my first.

"There is too much here," she said from the next, pulling out a wedge of notes, clearly more than the gardener should have been paid.

It quickly became apparent that all the counting errors had been mine and as soon as Maggie sorted out my envelopes the remaining cash balanced perfectly.

I decided not to help with payday the next month. Some things were just better left to the experts.

In the shade of the mulberry tree

There was a commotion in the corridor, people running and calls for Fortune to come. I left my desk to investigate. One of the secretaries had had a turn: she was shaking violently and staring with unseeing eyes. The other department heads were there: Leah and Joan were restraining her, Fortune was holding his hand out over her body. All were fervently praying. I heard their pleas for her deliverance, for her health, shouting out against the devil.

I dashed back to make a sugary tea, which was what I remembered being made for my father after a bad car accident, and took it through. The secretary had now calmed down, the fit had subsided but she was clearly pale and not yet fully aware of our presence. "Please, drink this," I said, passing the mug across. My colleagues – still praying – dismissed it, looking at me as if I was completely out of my mind.

I was ignored: neither wanted nor needed. My Western medical ethics were screaming, *Call for a doctor! Call for a doctor!* but my work colleagues simply carried on calling for the devil to leave the woman. This was a clash of cultures that I had not experienced to date. They were reliant on their faith, on God protecting their colleague, assured that the illness was the work of the devil and their zealous fervour could ban him from their presence. I was reliant on medicine, on highly intelligent, educated individuals analysing and diagnosing a problem, prescribing appropriate medicines to cure or alleviate symptoms. I was outnumbered and crept out of the room.

※

We had been praying for travelling mercies. Leah and the workers in her department were going to a project in the Choma District. It was many miles, a four-day trip. This neatly made a whole week off work, since everyone got a day off after travelling, even though they had a driver that took them everywhere. I could understand him needing a rest, but always questioned the other employees' need. However, I'd been shown the contracts and paperwork that spelled out what was expected and could not argue with their work practice. Privately, I suspected this was how some of my colleagues managed to maintain three jobs at once.

Leah came into the office to collect the project cash. While Winnie fetched the money from the safe she explained a bit more about the work she was doing. I was excited for her and the rest of the Women's Department. She was a formidable woman: comparatively elderly, having previously been a nurse and she still had an air of the matron about her. She always wore traditional African dress, although my eye was usually drawn to the wig of tight black curls that sat incongruously on her head. I had a lot of admiration for what she did, seeking to empower women and to educate about HIV/AIDS. The project in question was outreach to orphans and vulnerable children (OVCs). There were too many of them across the country. One estimate I'd heard was that of a population of eleven million, one million were orphaned children. This statistic was tempered by the fact that Zambians referred to children as orphans if they had lost just one parent; two parents made them a double orphan. Still, it remained a huge percentage.

AIDS had ravaged Zambia. No-one knew exactly how many had the disease, but Stephen's reflection that the Brought In Dead room opposite his lab was the busiest room in the hospital indicated how serious a problem it was. Estimates of HIV infection ranged from sixteen to thirty-five per cent, principally from looking at pregnant mothers who were routinely checked. The lower figure meant one in six people were HIV positive. Just within my office that would condemn half a dozen.

Leah explained they were taking food to poor families, to the elderly who were now responsible for bringing up grandchildren. They were teaching the need for abstinence, encouraging the women to be strong. "For all too often," she said with a shake of the head, "it is the men." She did not elaborate, for she was too polite and respectful. But her sigh spoke volumes. The culture was still very male dominated. Men who worked were entitled to their wages; wives and children often came a poor second after the pub and the girls. The man was head of the house: he could do as he pleased.

There was so little national testing that no-one could be sure who had and who had not got HIV/AIDS. The government was making valiant attempts to encourage people to be tested – even the Vice-President publicly had a test – but the disease was a death sentence, so why bother? No ordinary member of the population could ever afford the anti-retroviral drugs. The wealthy and prominent would simply disappear to South Africa and die 'of an illness'.

Meanwhile Leah and her women went into the compounds, into the villages and spoke of HIV, breaking the taboos, teaching the fundamentals. They cared for the members of society who were affected by it. The country as a whole was losing an entire generation: mine. The workers, the leaders and the parents were disappearing. How it would manage to sustain itself into the future was a mystery.

∽

I was driving home from work thinking of Maggie. She had come to me that day to ask for a loan.

"How much do you need?" I asked.

"One million kwacha," she replied. It was a lot of money, just shy of her full month's salary, and she was well-paid in local terms.

"OK, what do you need it for?"

"We need to pay the rent for three months."

"Haven't you just been paid?"

"Yes, but it does not cover this."

"How are you planning to repay it?"

"Three hundred thousand a month."

I did some simple calculations. This loan would not be paid off in three months. At that point she would need to pay another three months' rent, would come for another million and still be owing one hundred thousand.

As gently as I could I explained that I could not allow the repayment schedule she'd proposed. I was happy for her to have the loan (at least, as happy as I ever was to give an employer's advance) but she had to pay back at three hundred and fifty thousand a month.

Maggie's sunny face shadowed over. I could see I'd upset her and it broke my heart, for she was such a loving and honest woman. I asked how the money was spent, whether she had anything left over from her salary the previous week.

She listed out what had happened to it. Firstly there was the mealie meal and the charcoal. There was the electricity bill due and other money that was owed. The children's school fees had to be paid – the oldest two were on the site, but even the reduced employee's rates were a significant dent in her budget. The boy also needed shoes. There was childcare for her baby while she was at work, a measly sum paid to a teenage niece.

After she had listed everything out I realised that she had already spent more than her income, with another three weeks until payday and, of course, the rent money due.

I granted the loan, but was firm about my repayment schedule. My first responsibility was to the company. But as I turned into my driveway, looking at the home I comfortably rented on my husband's salary, I had to wipe a tear from my eye for Maggie and the thousands like her who from day to day had to make something out of nothing, had to feed and educate their children from a wage that barely maintained a standard of living for one adult.

THE SOLUTION TO MALNUTRITION: GOATS AND SUNFLOWERS

Richie was coming over for dinner and, since I had found kidney beans at the supermarket, I had splashed out on some tortillas and gone Mexican. Tortillas were an extravagance, but avocados were cheap and plentiful, so I had spent the afternoon making a guacamole according to the recipe book, with a few tweaks for the vagaries of Zambian produce. I'd even bought some mature cheddar cheese, although I was not convinced that it was any stronger than the normal stuff, just more expensive.

Richie arrived just as Stephen had finished Matthew's story and put out the light. I passed them both a Mosi and offered Richie a seat, before pouring

In the shade of the mulberry tree

myself some wine. They fell easily into conversation, Stephen letting off steam about his frustrations at work. Over the last six months I had heard these two discuss many of the problems they both faced in educating and feeding the poorest people in the country. Tonight was no different.

I placed the steaming vegetables on the table. We all tucked in, passing round the bowls of food. While helping himself to dip, Richie returned to the discussion about the children on the ward. "Presumably they get infection because of their malnutrition, so surely we have to solve the root cause: ensure they have food."

"Not all malnutrition is from not having food," Stephen replied.

I stopped with a tortilla halfway to my mouth. "I beg your pardon! Surely that's the definition of malnutrition – not having food?"

"Malnutrition means that you don't have enough of the right nutrients in the body. That can occur because there are too many leaving the body as much as because there are not enough going in," he explained. "That's why infection is such a key issue. Infection can cause diarrhoea and thus lead to malnutrition."

"So it is not just lack of food that is the problem. It is also the lack of appropriate food and the risk of diarrhoea, which will further reduce the body's nutrients, weaken their immune system and make them more susceptible to infection. It's a vicious circle!"

The triangle of malnutrition, infection and immunity seemed so interlinked yet it was unclear what the principal cause was. Does being malnourished weaken the immune system so that you get infection? Or does a poor immune system make you more prone to infection and therefore become malnourished? Or does infection weaken the immune system and bring on malnutrition?

The solution to malnutrition: goats and sunflowers

I wiped my mouth with a napkin and asked, "Do you want more? There's plenty in the kitchen."

I guessed the answer was yes from the wave of hands and mumblings that came through mouths full of food. Laughing, I went to the kitchen to warm some more tortillas and returned with the tub of yoghurt to replenish the bowl. I had tried to get sour cream but couldn't find any. My comment that I guessed sour cream was a luxury yet to reach Zambia was dismissed almost instantly.

"You can get sour milk," Richie stated.

"Really? Just as milk? Why on earth would you want that? We make quite enough of it in our house, leaving the milk bottle on the side after breakfast."

Both Richie and Stephen had experience of sour milk consumption at work. Stephen's nurses encouraged the children to drink it, presumably because they believed it to be easier on a weak stomach.

"Can't they get milk?" I asked naïvely. "Isn't that what we give children – full of all the nutrients that are needed? They could mix it with mealie meal to make decent porridge for the babies."

"Well, clearly that would be great, but do you know how much it costs?"

"It's what, about 15p for a bag of milk? Cheaper than Sainsbury's!" I blustered, before taking a large mouthful of tortilla wrap, juices dripping out of the sides.

"Yes, and how much do you pay your staff?"

Ah. Not so much that it would fund a pint a day on top of survival expenses. "Is the sour milk cheaper?" I eventually managed to ask.

"Perhaps it is, a bit. Still too expensive for most families to maintain when they go home. It is so frustrating!" Stephen gave a growl of anger and irritation. It was so maddening for him to work around the clock to save children's lives, only to send them home where the availability of food would, once more, be an issue.

Richie had been watching our conversation with wry amusement at my naïvety. Swallowing a mouthful he sat back in his chair, waved his fork slowly in the air and said, "I think the answer is goats." He put the fork down on his plate with a clatter.

"Goats?" We'd both stopped eating and looked at him in astonishment.

"Yes, goats."

We remained baffled. "Have another Mosi – I think you need it!" I joked. Richie accepted the bottle of beer but was adamant.

"I'm serious. Goats are the way forward."

"Why goats? Surely there are other sources of food?"

"Well, yes, but I wasn't thinking of eating them. I was thinking of milk goats."

"Ah!" Stephen was cottoning on faster. "A family with a goat has milk on demand."

"But why not get cows?" I asked.

There was another look of bemusement from the men. Clearly I had put my foot in it again. I was trying very hard to understand what Stephen did at work and this evening I was having a rapid lesson in animal production, human nutritional requirement and financing in the developing world. My brain was only just keeping up. I took a sip of wine, in case that helped.

"Price. Goats are a lot cheaper than cows. They don't require much in the way of upkeep – just look at the way they run around loose in the villages." Richie, the farmer, was warming to the subject. "Better still, cows need to calve annually in order to keep lactating but goats only need to have babies every two years."

The solution to malnutrition: goats and sunflowers

"So all we need to do is supply each mother with a milk goat and they'd be able to feed the children?"

"Yep! Or maybe two: a male would be required every two years!"

"And then there would be kids that would grow to provide more milk."

"Or income, if sold to another family or farmer."

Goats! Such a logical solution. Simple, easy to keep, cheap to maintain, providing enough milk daily for a family. Give a mother a milk goat and she could give her children the nutrients they needed for little cost. Could it catch on?

Finishing off the last of his tortilla Richie exclaimed, "That was delicious! Thanks, Catharine!"

"No worries!" I cleared away the debris of our main course, stacking plates and bowls precariously in the kitchen. I looked round somewhat despairingly: I really needed a bigger room. Though with less concrete, I decided. I opened the freezer and brought out desert.

"What is that?" Richie asked incredulously.

"Ice cream," I replied.

"No, not that, *that*." He pointed to the bowl beside the ice cream tub. In it was a brown sludge looking for all the world like hummus.

"Oh, that. Plumpy'nut."

"Plumpy'nut?"

"OK, well it isn't really Plumpy'nut: it is our experimental version – you are welcome not to have it. Stephen, you explain." I proceeded to scoop the vanilla ice cream into bowls while Stephen began.

"I heard of Plumpy'nut through the WHO course I did last month and have been searching for a recipe since. This is my attempt to reproduce it using local ingredients. It's a high energy protein food that I'm hoping may be an answer for my malnutrition dilemma."

In the shade of the mulberry tree

"So why are we eating it?" Richie asked wryly. It was a valid question.

I spooned some over the ice cream. "Someone has to be the guinea pig," I said. "We've already tried it with the children. Eleanor loves it. I think we can categorically state that she does not have a peanut allergy, given how much she consumed and spread all over her face."

Richie grinned at the image and turned back to Stephen. "So, what's in it? Nuts, clearly. Is that the energy or the protein?"

"Both, although the large quantity of icing sugar helps boost the energy intake. Basically it is ground nuts, icing sugar and oil."

"That's all?"

"Yes. We've pounded the ground nuts..."

"Ground ground nuts," I interjected, but my humour was brushed aside by the detailed explanation of the recipe. Stephen was enjoying talking about his ventures in the kitchen. I was less enthusiastic given he managed to burn out our food mixer grinding the nuts. We had resorted to asking Sherry to buy some nuts on her way home on Saturday, then pounding them for us and bringing the powder back with her to work on Monday.

"Erm, yes, and then I mixed it with the sugar and used enough oil for it to bind together into a, well, a lump. Go on – try it!"

Stephen waited expectantly. Richie dipped his spoon into the gloopy mess, taking a generous portion of ice cream and sauce. As he swallowed the rich mixture his eyes lit up.

"Wow! That's good! I wouldn't want much. But good!" He took another mouthful. Stephen and I laughed and dipped into our own portions. It was all

The solution to malnutrition: goats and sunflowers

that: very tasty, very sweet and delicious in small quantities.

"You see," said Stephen, "if we could make this affordable it would take no effort for the children to eat – it just melts on the tongue and would drip down into their stomachs."

As we ate we discussed further the potential production of Plumpy'nut. Peanuts grew well in Zambia and the town of Mazabuka was surrounded by sugar plantations. Stephen had used oil imported from South Africa, but it turned out that Richie not only had a passion for goats but also for sunflowers.

"Sunflowers! Why don't they grow sunflowers? There is sun and they can't need too much irrigation. I am sure that Zambians should be growing sunflowers. They can either eat the seeds or press them to make oil."

Sunflower oil should command a good price and was therefore potentially even more cost-effective to grow than maize and other crops. The flowers would also work well in the crop rotation mix, returning nutrients to the soil.

By the end of dinner we had solved all the problems of food security in Zambia. Local farmers just needed to rotate sunflowers, ground nuts and maize and they could provide themselves with all the nutrition they needed without having to buy expensive fertilisers. A couple of goats on the side, a few chickens running around and a family in a village could be self-sufficient, and healthy. When no more rich nutty sauce could be stomached, we chatted over coffee and, having duly set the world to rights, Richie stood to leave.

"Do you want a hand with the washing-up?" he asked.

"No, don't worry. Sherry will do it in the morning." I said. "What would I do without her?" I acknowledged silently to myself that my reliance on maids to do all the household chores was now complete.

After Richie'd left I took one final look at our kitchen, every surface covered with dirty plates and pots. I put a couple of dishes to soak and ensured all the leftovers were covered and put in the fridge. The rest was left for the ants and Sherry.

I switched off the light and went to bed.

THE BISHOP BLOWS AND THE POWER CUTS

At long last my father had arrived for a holiday.

"Hi Dad!" I stepped up to give him a welcoming kiss. "How was your journey?"

"Oh, fine," he said, while only partly meaning it. "I don't enjoy these overnight flights. I didn't sleep much. I'm getting too old, you know!"

I grinned at the thought of this. Into his seventies and he'd gladly ventured out here to visit while I, forty years his junior, had been filled with fear. He was still young enough for adventure. Taking the trolley from him I said, "I know, the lack of sleep is draining. But we haven't got anything planned for today so you are welcome to rest as much as you want."

I shooed away an over-enthusiastic porter who thought he'd get a few kwacha for helping with the luggage and I pushed Dad's trolley out of the terminal buildings into the glorious early morning sunshine. We chatted about trivialities until we reached The Bishop. I lifted the luggage in, slammed the door shut and climbed in to drive. Despite it only being 7.30 am I switched on the air-conditioning and eased the car out of the car park. My duty paid to the parking attendant, we settled down to drive back to our house.

"Welcome to Zambia," Dad read, peering ahead to the big arch over the road. "Thirty-nine years of independence. Gosh – you're going to have a big party next year then!"

"I guess so." The independence arch always seemed a little peculiar, set just after the police block near the airport and rising high above the road when there was nothing else around. It must have been a feat of engineering to make something that looks like stiff cardboard reach so high and withstand any winds that whistled across the plain.

I smiled at the languid policewoman guarding her oil drums and solitary road cone. She grimly waited for me to almost stop…before deciding that I was not a mass murderer, international terrorist, drug smuggler or whatever it was she was looking for and waved me on with her pristine white-gloved hands.

The vista through the arch was just a straight, long road and flat land covered in brown grass. I drove through and out onto the open road.

"How are Maggie's plans for the wedding?" I enquired. Since I left the UK six months ago my sister had met the man of her dreams and within a couple of months become engaged. While delightful, it was a bit of a surprise and I felt very distant from the whole relationship.

"They're looking at getting married next October, over half-term," he said, elaborating on some of the details about timing and venue. I interrupted every so often to point out some landmarks on the route. Finally we reached the home straight as I turned towards Kalingalinga.

Suddenly – bang!

I slammed on the brakes and the car skidded to a halt. The front left tyre had blown and I had created a lovely black stripe on the road behind me.

"I think the tyre's blown," said Dad, unhelpfully.

I took a deep breath and considered my options. There weren't many but at least I knew a good and reliable one. We had come to a halt just a hundred yards or so from EFZ: I was confident someone there would be able to change the tyre. The need for external help was not because I was an incompetent female driver who could not change a tyre, although I suspect I would never have been strong enough to turn those wheel nuts. No, the truth was more embarrassing: I knew I didn't have a wheel spanner or jack or any other tools in the back of the car. For some reason they hadn't come with The Bishop when we bought her, and I'd never got around to purchasing them. The Executive Director also drove a Pajero, and I was trusting that he would be in and amenable to helping his incompetent financial controller.

Several gentlemen appeared out of nowhere offering to help. Dad was delighted by their generosity of spirit but I wondered if they were simply expecting my (financial) generosity afterwards. Leaving Dad strict instructions not to move or do anything I ran to the offices for assistance.

I was not to be disappointed. As so often had been the case since my arrival in Zambia, Richie, with the assistance of one of the organisation's drivers, came to my aid.

"Welcome to Zambia," said Richie cheerfully to my father as they approached the car.

"Thank you," he replied. "I'm glad to be here – I think!"

❧

It was just past seven o'clock and everything was running a little late. Following the burst tyre the previous day I had had a stressful time driving into the centre of town to get the tyre replaced – mainly stressful as I only just had enough money. I hadn't realised just how expensive tyres would be for a four-wheel drive. I took the opportunity to purchase a wheel nut spanner and jack, so our upcoming drive to Livingstone was expected to be a little safer.

Stephen had run in from the car, dripping wet. It may have been only a short distance to the door but in a tropical rainstorm it was quite long enough to get soaked through. He dried himself down in the kitchen, dripping all over the floor. I wished he wouldn't as he was in the way as I put the finishing touches to dinner. I was running late: the children should already have been in bed.

"How was your day?" I asked him.

"Oh, fine," he sighed, "just four admissions and three deaths."

I smiled sympathetically. Any child's ill health was upsetting for him, particularly when it was so avoidable.

"Did you get a chance to see Mutende?"

"Yes. She's had the rest of her chemotherapy course. She looks dreadful though."

"I'm so glad Daniel was able to get the drugs from Zim." Mutende had been on my mind a lot lately and I worried for her and Daniel. I kept thinking of extra bits of furniture that I might purchase from him to help fund her healthcare.

"Me too." Stephen busied himself with the towel, but I could tell he was avoiding the conversation.

There was a click as the kettle switched off and I squeezed past him to get to it. "Can you start setting the table and call everyone for dinner?"

With the kitchen to myself again I warmed Eleanor's food and carried the casserole bowl through.

"Bean surprise!" I exclaimed with delight. Matthew pulled a face, Dad looked on apprehensively and Stephen busied himself with finding a bib for Eleanor. I ignored them all and served up. While Matthew prodded his plateful hoping to find a longed-for fish finger, I sat down to eat.

As if my action had pressed the off-switch, we were plunged into darkness. A couple of seconds later Matthew screamed.

While not the first time that ZESCO had unexpectedly cut the power, this was the first time it had happened at night with the children still awake. Of course, with her brother screaming, Eleanor followed suit and no matter what their mum and dad said about not worrying, it was only when the candles were lit that the noise was hushed. The five of us finally settled down to dinner by candlelight.

༄

The following evening Stephen's supervisor came to dinner. He had flown in from the UK that morning, spent the day with Stephen coming to grips with all the permutations of the virology lab, and I was in charge of impressing the boss with a sumptuous evening meal.

At 7 pm the lights went again. It was just fifteen minutes before he was due to arrive, but pasta didn't cook on warm air.

No electricity, no cooking, no hot meal. We grovelled to Richie who thankfully came over to babysit while we went out for steaks courtesy of a restaurant with a generator. Stephen's supervisor bluffed his way into the eatery, which always required you to pre-book, telling the waiter that he was only in town for the one night (true) and had heard that this was the best restaurant (probably also true) and he really wanted to eat here — surely they could find a table for four somewhere without us having to wait a further hour? I was astonished by his audacity. It was a very un-British trait, something I would never be bold enough to attempt. But he was originally from South Africa, and was buzzing with being back on his home continent. Sure enough, five minutes later we were sitting down and he had ordered T-bone steak and pepper sauce.

⚘

The next night I cooked dinner early and lit the candles at 7 pm. The lights went out ten minutes later and this time we were all prepared. Another re-setting of the electrical alarm clock at bedtime and our rainy season routine was established.

RUNNING ON EMPTY

My father's visit had given us an excuse to explore new parts of Zambia. I had booked us all to stay for a week in Kasanka National Park over Christmas. Kasanka is known for its bat migration at this time of year and it is one of the most fascinating natural occurrences, unique to Zambia. But firstly we were visiting the most popular tourist destination in the country: we were going to Livingstone to see the Victoria Falls.

Stephen took a Friday off work to give us enough time over the weekend to both travel and appreciate the sights. We took the 500 kilometre drive south from Lusaka in The Bishop, anticipating a relaxing two-night stay in a chalet by the river. A journey of this length enabled us to appreciate all the comforts of our four-wheel drive – not for its off-road capabilities but for its air-conditioning and well-sprung seats. Matthew got the rich privilege of being right at the back on one of the fold-down seats, surrounded by suitcases. My father took the front seat, for the view and leg space. Stephen and I alternated between driving and the back-seat role of entertaining Eleanor.

The drive took us through the sugar plantations of Mazabuka, the fishing districts around the Kafue and the agricultural land of Monze and Choma. We'd had an early start and stopped in Monze for lunch, pulling over beside a café designed for lorry drivers rather than expat families. I was paranoid someone would steal our belongings from the roof rack and refused to go far from the car. Stephen pointed out that everything was covered in tarpaulin and tied securely with rope so he wasn't quite sure how a chancing thief would manage to snaffle anything. Nevertheless, my unease won and we were all restricted to egg rolls and greasy sausages.

At about four o'clock we reached Kalomo and Stephen drove into the BP station with about an eighth of a tank left. Switching off the engine, he breathed a big sigh of relief. We'd been travelling for seven hours with only a break for lunch and toilet stops for the potty-training three-year-old. We were all exhausted and, while my children's behaviour had, for the most part, been excellent, they were becoming a little fractious. Some diesel here and then we'd be off on the final leg of our journey – surely less than an hour to go.

While Stephen took a swig from the water bottle I noticed the petrol attendant waving at us. Stephen opened the window.

"No diesel, bwana," he said.

My heart sank.

"No diesel?"

"No. We're expecting a delivery."

Aha! Hope! It was late afternoon. Surely it couldn't be long?

"When will it come?"

"Sometime, sir. It is on its way."

We looked at him, and at the petrol gauge, and at each other, and gave a collective sigh. We'd been in Zambia long enough to know what 'sometime' meant. There was no way we could guarantee the delivery in anything less than twenty-four hours. We had little diesel left and a further 100 kilometres to go. At a guess we had done 400 kilometres on about 70 litres: would the final ten litres stretch the distance? We were all worn out and the children were fed up. What choice did we have? We bade the attendant a falsely cheery farewell, started the engine and left.

It was my turn to drive and I watched the gauge assiduously, fearing a plummet to 'E'. The Bishop was a fantastic vehicle, but its age was clearly evident in some areas, one of which was the unreliability of lights on the dashboard. I realised we were testing for the first time whether the light that came on when the fuel was low actually worked.

My mind was racing, flooded with questions. Expecting disaster at any moment I mentally planned ahead. Could we camp in the car? Could there possibly be other fuel stations? The next town was Zimba. Was that a town of any size and merit? If we did stop or breakdown, who would help us? Was it closer to go back, or to go forwards?

There was a game of intellectual one-upmanship going on around me, as my father and husband tried to work out what speed I should drive at in order to economise best on fuel.

"Magazine adverts give the mpg based on a speed of 55 mph," my father chipped in.

"Miles per gallon?" Stephen queried. "The Bishop travels in kilometres. And litres of diesel."

"Well," Dad backtracked, dismissing this newfangled nonsense with a wave of his hands, "whatever it is nowadays."

There was a brief silence as the gentlemen competed to do the sums. "So, 55 mph is about 80-90 kph," my father approximated quickly. He won the race.

"Or 88.5 kph," my husband couldn't resist throwing in just seconds later. He won on accuracy. I laughed. The higher mathematics had killed time and relieved tension. As far as possible I kept to that speed.

My high hopes for Zimba came and went, and our steady pace in fifth gear was ruined by the atrocious state of the road after leaving the town. The journey through failing light avoiding potholes was very stressful. We passed a couple of road works, but all the evidence was that these were just patching up and unlikely to survive the imminent rains.

Periodically my father extended his neck to have a look at the fuel gauge. This was rather annoying and didn't do my stress levels any good. The big 'E' was reached but Livingstone was not in sight. The car kept moving so clearly there was some generosity from the tank. Stephen re-read books to Matthew and Eleanor, while in my anxiety I was panicking like mad.

A dreadful thought struck me: what if the garage in Livingstone was waiting for the same fuel tanker as in Kalomo?

Still there was no warning light on the dashboard.

Out of nowhere I spotted a couple of oil drums in the middle of the road: a police block. I let out a little whoop of joy. A police block surely meant civilisation; and that had to mean we were approaching Livingstone. Never had seeing the police been greeted with such relief; rarely had I smiled so broadly at them; nor been so happy to hand over my passport, driving licence and insurance documents. We rolled into Livingstone, presumably surviving on air more than fuel, gently trundling over a road of sleeping policemen before pulling in at the first garage we saw. Thankfully it hadn't yet shut for the night.

There was only one obstacle left to overcome.

"Do you have diesel?" I asked the attendant tentatively, dreading the worst.

The man beamed and with a small tilt of his head to the side said, "Certainly Madam – how much do you want?"

✺

Just as the sun had set we arrived at Miramba River Lodge, relieved to have finally made it. The children were delighted to bounce out of the car and run around. We were treating ourselves to chalets, with the excuse that a chalet would be best for my father. We weren't prepared to pay for the westernised luxuries of the Zambezi Sun and Royal Livingstone hotel complex next door. In addition to their chalets, Miramba offered safari tents and camping facilities, both of which looked excellent, as well as its own restaurant and swimming pool, but the hook that reeled us in was that it had a children's play area.

Matthew spotted it immediately and made a beeline for the wooden climbing frame. Being past sunset my mind thought *snakes!* but I was drawn away to register at reception and then to persuade the chef to stay on a little longer to feed us. The resulting meal was disappointing and, rather than eat there again, we decided to make use of the braai stand outside our chalet for the evening meal the following day.

However, our meagre camping equipment was insufficient for anything close to a cooked meal. We had come prepared for breakfast (cereal and UHT milk) and snacks (biscuits, drinks, crisps). We were totally ill-equipped for cooking meat and vegetables. Knives? Chopping board? Tongs? Charcoal? Rather than the longed-for visit to the Victoria Falls the morning brought a trip to the supermarket.

Shoprite was the main supermarket chain around Zambia and at that time the only one in Livingstone. We set off in The Bishop confident of finding it. After all, Livingstone was not a large town and Shoprite's sign was unmissable. After ten minutes of driving up and down the main street looking for its bright orangey-yellow logo with large, red lettering we gave up and asked for directions. Following them to the letter we still could not find the shop. We were baffled, as the big 'S' symbol was usually everywhere. Eventually we found it down a side street. Being waved into a tight space by a local I commented cynically, "We should have known it was here – there is nowhere to park."

Inside, the shop was small and cramped compared with the one I was used to in Lusaka. There were long queues at the bread counter, a spacious area for fresh food and then just three or four short aisles for everything else. Buying the food was easy, but the equipment was a lengthy list. The cheap evening meal became a logistical nightmare and our limited cash funds were not helping. Still we bravely told ourselves this was a good investment, we would use everything again and nothing would be wasted.

We left the shop and returned to The Bishop with our provisions. There were a couple of boys hanging around her. My paranoia grabbed hold again – what were they attracted to? Too many stories of car theft or break-ins had left me suspicious of anyone taking an interest in my vehicle.

"What are you doing?" I asked sternly.

"Cleaning the car, Madam," he replied. At this point I noticed the cloth and bucket, the windscreen wipers pointing to the sky. I was aware that following our long drive yesterday she was not the cleanest of vehicles, but I also knew this boy was not wasting precious water for the good of his own health.

"Did I ask you to do this?" I enquired.

"But, Madam, the car is dirty."

I raised an eyebrow.

"See, Madam, the glass is clear. Come, Madam, have a look," he gestured eagerly, extending an arm to encourage me to be impressed by his handiwork. I had to be fair to him: he had done a good job. We now had a beautifully clean vehicle, which would be beneficial for our journey home the next day. I sighed and put our food in the back. We strapped in the children and all clambered in, while the boy continued to extol his achievements, at my heel like a persistent terrier with a postman.

As I climbed into the driver's seat, the long-expected happened: the hand was cupped and he tapped on the side window, a long, sad face with droopy, pleading eyes. "Please, Madam, something." As I sighed, looked to Stephen and delved into my bag for change, the begging continued. "Please, Madam, I'm hungry. Please, some kwacha, please."

I passed him some small change and his face was transformed with a beaming smile. "Thank you, Madam, thank you," he said, cupping his hands and softly clapping them together while bowing his head, a sign of gratitude and humility. Despite resenting paying for something I hadn't asked for, I couldn't help but smile back and thank him.

'GAZED UPON BY ANGELS IN THEIR FLIGHT'

Known locally as *Mosi-oa-Tunya*: the smoke that thunders, the Victoria Falls are one of the greatest natural wonders of the world. Although neither the highest nor widest waterfalls in the world, they claim to be the largest based on the wall of water that falls: a width of 1.7 kilometres and a height of 108 metres forms what may be the largest sheet of falling water. No other waterfalls are both wider and higher. Spanning the Zambezi River between Zambia and Zimbabwe, David Livingstone first discovered them in 1855 (hence the name of the town on the Zambian side). Livingstone approached them from upstream, landing his canoe on an island in the middle of the river. From there he had his first view of the vertiginous drop, peeking over the edge, writing later in his diary: "Scenes so lovely must have been gazed upon by angels in their flight."

Our approach was a lot tamer but no less stunning. Leaving our lodge, we drove round close to the border post. We parked alongside all the other tourists near the small tollbooth at the entrance to the World Heritage Site. We had been told that we could hire raincoats here, but the raincoat building was firmly shut. We'd come so far that we decided to grit our teeth and just get soaked. We followed the path through the trees towards the gentle rumbling noise. There was no sign of anything but the lush green foliage, a mini-rainforest maintained by the drifting spray. Down a few steps to a viewpoint and the noise level rose exponentially. At long last we were treated to a full-length view of the Falls.

Nothing comes close to describing the impact of all that water rushing over the precipice. The noise was indeed thunderous, the spray was refreshing as the sun rose in the sky, the rainbows were clear and abundant, changing position and ferocity with the angle of the sun. Waterfalls are naturally mesmerising, such that I could stand and look at them for hours. But we'd only just started our adventure: expectantly we moved on.

Continuing on the path we took a deviation through the vegetation on our left and found a stunning view of the railway bridge. This was the border point between Zambia and Zimbabwe and Matthew was delighted to see a train on the bridge. Presumably customs and immigration was being done on board, as it was stopped there for some time. We heard the occasional toot and Matthew's excitement reached fever pitch on seeing black smoke come from the engine. With a final whistle and puff of smoke it moved on into Zimbabwe, chuffing its way over the bridge to track its way through to Victoria Falls town and beyond.

"Can I wait for another one, Mum?" Matthew asked. Laughing, I had to explain that I was not sure that there was more than one train a day and we certainly weren't hanging around to wait for the next.

It was not much further to the knife-edge bridge. The name was apt. Its metal frame spanned a precipitous dip in the land to a further outcrop that was longing to be an island. I couldn't quite get my head around who might have thought of the idea of constructing it in the first place. It was just below the height of the Falls and from both bridge and land we got to view the waterfalls face on. Mist rose into the sky, partially from water evaporation, partially from the force of hitting the rocks and rising up. It was December: the effect of the rains had yet to reach here, replenishing the Zambezi from the north of the country, and our fears about waterproofs were unfounded. Instead we were privileged to see the strata of the rocks behind the water and trickles dribbling down. We stared down into the abyss, mesmerised by the swirling waters and rapids, then looked up and identified the island on which Livingstone had stood.

Cautiously edging our way around the perimeter of the buttress we gazed at the waterfall at its weakest point in the year. It was considered a wonder of the world for a reason: it was impossible not to marvel at the creation of such beauty and fearful force in one package.

Walking back to the car we took a small detour upstream. Within a hundred metres the noise level dropped to a steady drumming hum. The peace and quiet was amazing. Local people were washing themselves and their clothes in the river: indeed some were walking across the top of the Falls and I was grateful my children were not yet at an age to consider that a dare. People were picnicking in a small, sandy hollow where in April there would be the swirling waters of the Zambezi in full flow.

It was with reluctance that we trekked back to the car park, while Eleanor waved happily from her vantage point on Stephen's back and Matthew excitedly rushed ahead in anticipation of ice cream.

∾

As this could have been Dad's only trip to the Victoria Falls (and I didn't think he was really into the bungee jumping, gorge swinging, white water rafting and microlights) we went to investigate the much advertised helicopter flights over the valley and Falls. Taking a left off the road onto a dirt track we wound our way over the railway line and through dusty bush, up an incline to the helipad and visitor centre. All the boy's hard work outside Shoprite that morning was gone in an instant as the white Bishop became dusty orange.

While I unpacked the children, the men went to see if there was anyone available to help us. The reception area was a magnificent building, with decking stretching out over the edge of the hill. From there, anxiously keeping the crawling Eleanor and excitable Matthew from the edge, I was able to look out over the landscape. The late afternoon sun was beaming down, reflecting on the river, easily identifiable by the plumes of mist rising from the waterfalls. In front of me was stony, craggy land with a light covering of bushy trees, a few bright green leaves of new growth following recent rains. In the distance were mountains, the beginnings of Zimbabwe and beyond that Botswana: countries for another day, another visit.

I turned on hearing my name called.

"Catharine, do you want to go in a helicopter?"

"Yes, please!" I replied enthusiastically. I'd never been in a 'copta', as Matthew would say, and having seen this view I couldn't help but think it would be amazing.

"It's $160 each," Stephen said.

Ah, twice the price of bungee jumping. Longer period of enjoyment, I would imagine, but nevertheless very expensive. But it was a once-in-a-lifetime experience.

"Apparently there's a flight available at four o'clock with two people booked on it, but it will only go if there are four," Stephen continued. "If we aren't interested they will phone the hotel where the others are staying and cancel."

Guilt was added to greed. Dad would love to go; these other visitors wanted to go. One of us would have to stay on the ground with the children: even if they were allowed to fly our budget certainly wasn't stretching to tickets for them too. Over Stephen's shoulder I could see a big screen showing a film of the flight, down the gorge over rapids and between rocks and boulders; soaring high over the misty falls; views of the landscape all around. Surely this was worth the money?

I looked at Stephen. "Let's do it," I blurted out. But which of us was going to get the flight, and who had the children? As I pulled the long straw and accompanied my father on a helicopter flight I realised that I was going to have some serious payback later.

Inside the cockpit we were firmly strapped in and each had headphones with microphones, so we could hear the pilot and ask him any questions we had. Above us the blades started to whirr and I quickly saw how little you would hear without this technology. I had a seat by the window on the right-hand side and waved to

'Gazed upon by angels in their flight'

the children. They had thirty minutes to entertain their father.

Flying over the area inhabited by the paramount chief, Chief Sekuti, we could see the zigzag shape of the river in front of us. The Victoria Falls originally began several miles downstream from their current location, as water fell over the edge of the escarpment. Over time the water found a fault or weak point further back in the surface of the plateau, which started to wear away beneath the gallons of water flowing over it, until eventually the whole fissure cracked open and collapsed, creating a new waterfall almost perpendicular to the first. This process had been repeated eight times, creating the zigzag gorge over three miles long through which we were dramatically flown. Below were the rapids, where some foolhardy people were white-water rafting – undoubtedly an amazing experience but a little too close to crocodiles for my comfort. At rapid 25 there was a helipad constructed to help anyone who got into serious distress: other than that there was little land, a lot of churning water and rock walls up to 140 metres high.

The helicopter rose up and our next points of interest were the Falls themselves, as we flew a 'figure of eight' over the gushing water. From the sky the volume of water flooding over the Zimbabwean side was clear to see, as were the beginnings of the next gorge as the water wore its way through the weakening rock. It will look very different in a thousand years' time! From the air the islands dotting the upstream river were clear, as was the 108 metre drop into the first gorge. The only way out for the millions of litres of water that fall every second at peak periods was through the 110 metre gap in the rock that we had looked across when on foot earlier. Waters swirled ferociously below, before rushing into the second gorge spanned by the railway bridge linking Zambia and Zimbabwe.

The pilot took us on a final loop a short distance upstream, returning to base by flying over Mosi-oa-Tunya National Park. We had to fly high so as not to distress the animals, which also meant I could not spot them. The pilot told us there were elephants marching through but for me they were lost in the scrub, rock and dust.

Arriving back at the helipad there were two young, wild animals easily spotted, rushing to greet their mother…and their drained father, who no doubt was thinking he really should have gone on the helicopter ride instead.

༄

After returning to our lodge we ventured over to the pool for a quick dip before we began dinner. The pool was warm, refreshing after our day in the humid heat of the Zambezi valley. There was a small shallow area where Eleanor could splash about while Matthew swam bravely with his armbands on around the surprisingly deep pool. It was the first we'd seen with navy-blue tiling inside, presumably using the dark colour to help trap the warmth of the sun in the water. With the late afternoon rays beating down on my body, I enjoyed a brief moment lazing on a sun lounger. I knew it would be the calm before the storm that was dinner and bedtime. It dawned on me that we hadn't slopped on the sun-block. Eyes closed, I heard the children laughing and giggling, the splashing water and the banter with their father. I lifted my head and opened one eye: no, right now the peace was more important than the argument.

Back at the chalet Stephen lit the braai and went into protective-male (or knowledgeable-medic) mode, surrounding the area with mosquito coils. These burn slowly over a matter of hours and deter mosquitoes from coming close. Inside I followed the daily routine to cover the children with anti-mosquito spray. The best way to avoid malaria was not to be bitten in the first place. More coils were placed in the bedroom area, nets were lowered.

We sat at a picnic bench outside our chalet. I knew from earlier that we were looking out to a field of trees that surrounded the camp, but now the view was black: a faint shadow of tree branches could just be made out, waving against the inky night sky. We could hear the distant rumble of the waterfalls and, closer to hand, the crickets and cicadas. A branch snapped: what animals were out there? It was impossible to see or to know. There were likely to be monkeys or baboons, which would later come in search of the scraps from our meal, but perhaps we had heard a hippo moving from the river for its night-time graze, or an elephant on its way to ransack a local villager's crops.

After nearly three years of not talking, Matthew had at last got the hang of sentences and questions. Enlivened by his incessant chatter we tucked into burgers and sausages, roughly hacked bread (a bread knife would have been useful) and generous squirts of tomato ketchup. Not exactly *cordon bleu*, but a satisfying meal with no complaints from the children.

Replete, Matthew and Eleanor were encouraged to bed. Back outside, I settled down with my husband and father to finish off the bottle of wine in peace. But conversation was muted as we enjoyed the stillness of the night air. Looking up I could see the stars and, not for the first time, wondered what they were. I recalled the North Star, the Bear and Orion with his belt from my childhood attempts using an 'I Spy' book, but living in the southern hemisphere I realised that the North Star was not likely to be my guiding light.

Daylight past, exhaustion overwhelming, we bade each other goodnight and retreated to the cocooning world of our beds. Safely tucked up under net and sheets, I drifted into sleep, lulled by the gently whirring overhead fan and rested for the journey home the next day.

PEL'S FISHING OWL

Zambia is shaped a little like a butterfly or a squashed figure of eight. Or perhaps the symbol for infinity: certainly her roads seemed to stretch on to infinity and, once more, we were travelling their vast length, this time to the North of the country. After the trip to Livingstone, and the escapade on the way home from the airport with my father, we had learnt our lesson: this time round we not only had the appropriate toolkit for a burst tyre but were also stopping frequently for fuel.

Unfortunately, timing the journey was a lesson yet to be perfected. We'd just passed Serenje and the sun was sinking in the sky. According to our directions we were still 90 kilometres short of our destination: Kasanka National Park. As we would be staying a long way from anywhere, the arrangement with the lodge was that we brought the raw ingredients with us and their chefs would prepare and cook them. It was quite a feat to plan all our consumables for a week and load them into The Bishop, together with clothes, travel cot, nappies, Christmas presents, birthday presents for Matthew and all the toys required to entertain our children.

Having been on the road since early morning we were tired, hungry and bored. Foot down, I raced over the hills, desperate to reach the gate before it closed at 18 hours. I sent up prayers of gratitude for the Romans and the Chinese influence over this highway, since the road was largely straight and had very few potholes. With barely five minutes to spare, I pulled up at the gate.

I breathed a sigh of relief that we had arrived and would now have a bed for the night. Joy was short-lived, as the nappy that should have been dealt with half an hour earlier could not be deferred any longer. An emergency change on the gravel outside the guard's post reminded me of the exploding nappy at Paddington Railway station just six months before, only this was much smellier. When all was cleaned up, the car and its inhabitants signed in, we more sedately drove the twelve kilometre track to the main reception at Wasa Camp.

We had booked to stay our first couple of nights in their other camp at Luwombwa Lodge. Checking that we still wanted to go there, the receptionist radioed ahead to ensure the pontoon was still in operation. It was, but as darkness was falling there was no time to waste. She told us it was on the road out of the site, and we were off again.

We took the track the receptionist indicated with the wave of her arm, in a general direction through the buildings. Night was falling, the skies were leaden-grey, a murky twilight. Clear of the lodge, we passed across a misty plain littered with rocky termite mounds, looking eerily like tombstones. In the growing gloom I drove gingerly around the spooky graves.

"I'm not sure this is the right way." Perhaps it was the ghostly atmosphere, perhaps payback for the hair-raising drive of the previous couple of hours or maybe exhaustion, but at the pit of my stomach I felt the route to be wrong.

"We came the way she pointed," Stephen responded, "and we can't go far wrong."

I was less confident and immensely grateful when we reached a T-junction with a track that looked more robust. However the receptionist had given no indication that we would have to make a decision about which direction to take. We made a guess but my peace of mind only returned when we passed some guards, camped around a fire to keep warm in the damp night. At least someone was available to redirect us if we found our guess was incorrect.

I hardly had time to think that when the track we were on disappeared under a river not ten metres away. I slammed on the brakes.

The Kasanka River was not wide and the pontoon was little more than a bunch of oilcans tied together with rope. It had none of the solidity of the Kafue pontoon we'd crossed back in August. Then Matthew had screamed. Would that happen again? I glanced in the rear-view mirror. He was still awake, but seemed oblivious.

I stared back at the river. How did we deal with this? There was no sign of any help. Stephen was just about to get out and do all the hard work himself when one of the men from the scout post came running up behind us. His halting English combined with my tiredness meant the conversation took some time to unravel. He gestured as to where I should drive.

Apparently the oilcans, planks and string really were strong enough to take our heavily-laden four-by-four.

My heart in my mouth, I drove The Bishop onto the pontoon. The guard seemed happy with our positioning and we were off. Unlike crossing the Kafue, there was no mechanical aid, no winch or wheel to wind. It was just brute force and incredible strength from the guide, as he heaved on the rope to guide the pontoon across to the other side.

Coming to the opposite bank we were faced by a steep, muddy path. At eye level all I could see was a wall of orange mud. With speed it might seem feasible to mount it but we were starting from stop.

"How on earth am I supposed to get up there?" I asked.

"Four-wheel drive?" suggested Stephen.

I didn't naturally think of that as an option, so there were a couple of minutes while I negotiated the second gear stick. There were no labels on it (another quirk of The Bishop) but after a couple of moves a green light appeared on the dashboard. Given The Bishop's temperamentality in this area I could not guarantee the two events were linked. With no confidence at all I revved up to mount the bank. An uncomfortable scrape came from the back of the car but we weren't stopping, and after a few eternal seconds I safely reached the top of the hill and the riverside road to camp.

"What was the noise?" I asked Stephen, as we waved goodbye to the pontoon man.

"I don't know," he replied cautiously, "probably just the bumper."

I glanced anxiously at him.

"Ah well, that's what it's there for," Dad said from the back. By this reasoning we could bump anyone out of a parking space or persistently reverse into walls, but I didn't have time to philosophise.

"Are we there yet?" called Matthew.

"Nearly, nearly," I replied more cheerily than I felt. "Not far to go now!"

It was now pitch black and the rain had started to fall. I drove over the rocky track, hoping that we were heading in the right direction. Our journey to get that far had hardly been faultless and now I didn't have the daylight benefit of visual clues. After a few minutes of being gentle with the vehicle, I decided to put my rally driving expertise to the test. I was still in four-wheel drive and I raced along the muddy track, dodging the biggest dips. Branches scraped along the length of the vehicle but I was motivated by the prospect of a G&T, dinner and bed.

I arrived at our destination exhausted and worn out. My legs were wobbly as I stepped out from the car following a good twelve hours on the road. The back door of The Bishop was unexpectedly stiff but with a sharp tug it came open and our luggage was unloaded. The camp guards showed us to our family chalet and, having argued with Matthew over who slept where, we returned to the communal area for a quick supper that the chef concocted for us. In the dark we could see nothing of our environment and we collapsed into bed, hoping that the journey was worth it.

∽

It was. Stephen and I woke to see the Luwombwa River snaking past our spacious chalet. As the first rays of sunlight sparkled on the water, a kitchen help brought hot tea and coffee to the terrace, where we relaxed and enjoyed the view for a few moments before the children woke.

We were the only guests and the peace was palpable. The morning air was fresh and bracing, a clear blue sky and rising sun portending a hot day ahead. There were birds singing, trees rustling. At breakfast in the central camp dining area we could hear peals of laughter from the workers' kitchen after an animated conversation, pans clanging as their morning shift finished.

Our chief host and guide came over to our table. "What would you like to do today?" he asked. "Game drive? Fishing? Canoe?"

I looked to Stephen and Dad.

"We don't need to do everything at once." Dad had clearly settled comfortably into the Zambian pace of life. Stephen backed him up, emphasising that we did have a whole week, albeit in the two locations in the park, so we could take it easy.

I was more pragmatic. "After yesterday, I'd really appreciate a day without driving. I think my bum would appreciate being moulded into a different shape than that of the driver's seat in The Bishop."

After more debate, we chose to take a leisurely canoe trip up the river.

We passed by The Bishop to see what damage she had incurred. Daylight gave no evidence of scratches down the side, for which I was greatly relieved as there had been some close shaves as we'd sped along the track.

"Does the bumper look funny to you?"

"Hmm…" Stephen was eyeing it carefully, "it's a bit higher on the right-hand side. And was the mudflap always like that?"

It was hanging off slightly. Clearly the incident at the pontoon had caused a bit more damage than we'd imagined. Stephen and Dad fiddled with the bumper and then tried opening the back door. There was still a slight scraping noise as it passed over the metal step but otherwise all seemed OK.

"It'll get us home." Dad dismissed the problem. I wandered back to our chalet to pack for the day feeling more concerned about The Bishop's impending garage bill.

∾

The canoes were not large enough for all of us so Dad and Stephen got one, while I followed on child monitoring duty in the second. As I climbed into the canoe my reservations began. I'd not liked sitting in small boats ever since a family punting trip along the river at Stratford when a teenager. My father was in control, supposedly. He was probably much better and safer than I remember but we nearly ran into other punters and I found the whole journey tense, embarrassing and hugely uncomfortable.

My personal fears and inhibitions were compounded by the realisation that perhaps small, narrow boats were not the best option for a crawling one-year-old, trying hard to walk, and a boisterous three-year-old boy. There were no such things as life jackets, but then what use would they be in crocodile infested waters? However, the decision had been made and I counter-argued its merits to myself. After all, in principle a boat seemed to be quite containing: the children couldn't go anywhere. *Except overboard* the devil inside my mind shouted back.

The guides pushed off from the side and for a while we settled down and enjoyed the peace and quiet. The day was warming up and the silence hung heavily over the water, broken by the gentle lapping of the river against the banks and the paddles hitting the water in a steady rhythm. Once more I was struck by the immense strength and control of these local men as we punted upstream.

We seemed to be heading towards a plain. To our left and ahead was the unmistakable yellow-orange of dry grass and open landscape. A few trees grew beside the river, drinking up the water to flourish in abundant green. The guide, standing up as he punted the canoe along, saw antelope on the distant plain, but they were not visible from our seats low in the boat.

We turned round a bend in the river and the scene changed. Now plant life closely surrounded the river: an avenue of green as the bushes leaned over to kiss each other and the taller trees stretched to the sky. Occasional sandy breaks revealed drinking holes for the animals and sunlit spots for the sleeping crocodiles.

There was an unexpected plop in the water and we turned to the guide.

"Fish," he said, smiling, and carried on paddling steadily, all the time scouring the river bank.

Suddenly the man in front stopped paddling and looked intently into a bush at the side. He said something in Bemba to his colleague, our guide. The children were shushed and reluctantly respected the silence. We drew close and joined in the search: for what, we did not know.

"Pel's fishing owl," whispered the guide. Slowly, painfully, he directed us to the bird: a brown owl sitting in the brown branches of a tree on a bank of brown earth. We were impressed, not because of the bird (which was a large bird of prey) but because they were able to spot this creature in the middle of a mass of foliage. We showed suitable awe and eagerly expected a boat trip overwhelmed by bird-spotting.

It was a foolish expectation. The children, quite interested in the expedition for the first half hour, became restless. A secret box of goodies was uncovered from my bag, postponing the inevitable. Gradually the volume levels from our boat rose and, combined with the increasing heat, the birds steered well clear of us. Even the crocodiles were only heard, not seen: the quiet swoosh and then gentle splash as they glided from the banks to the river's depths. The animals stayed in the shade and clearly had sufficient watering holes still available on land to not need to come down to the river to drink. We returned to camp with several sightings of a fish eagle swooping overhead and a few common birds twittering amongst the bushes but little else to write home about.

∽

In the evening we were stilled once again by the beauty of Africa. Children asleep, we stepped outside to witness the most magnificent sunset, an orange sky spread out before us, trees silhouetted against its vibrant colour. There was little sound, as all the creatures settled down for the night and the owl hooted his way over the river looking for prey. This was Africa at its most glorious: unrivalled Mother Nature being bigger and greater than anything mere mortal man could achieve.

BETTER BATTING FIRST

The next day we packed up and travelled back to Wasa Lodge. Like the Wise Men, we returned by a different route, taking a bridge over the Kasanka River upstream from the pontoon. Daylight made the whole journey much more pleasant. Winding through the forest, we keenly looked out for birds, antelope or more exciting creatures. Belatedly we realised that the benefit of fresh air blowing through The Bishop was far outweighed by the pain of being thoroughly chewed by the tsetse flies that got into the car. Too late we closed the windows and turned the air-conditioning on.

By now flies were everywhere. Stephen, in the back with the children, was worst affected not only because they found him particularly tasty but also because he had to deal with the children's wails when they were bitten. Stephen wrapped them both up in blankets to reduce the risk; the air-conditioning went full blast at freezing to compensate. To lighten the mood Stephen introduced a competition to see who could kill the most. Matthew made vain waving attempts before retreating back under the blanket. Now that the flies were trapped in the car, they buzzed up against the windows, fighting for the daylight and trees outside. Perfect: take aim… Splat! Stephen squashed them into the corners in record numbers. I couldn't win as I was driving and my father got bonus points for the bloodiest smear on the passenger's window. That fly had clearly filled himself up on one of us. I bet it was my blood, I thought, leaning down to scratch my ankle.

∽

The main camp overlooked a small lake, partially hidden by an expanse of marshy reed beds. Our rondavel was pleasantly furnished with a small balcony in front and we were just a short walk from the main buildings. It was here that we settled down for the afternoon in comfortable chairs on the large veranda, to rest, unwind and to put together a more organised plan for the rest of the holiday. Dad was having a break from our familial noise, recovering in his chalet from the tsetse fly battle. Stephen was busy entertaining Matthew with a series of jigsaws at the table while Eleanor banged at some toys on the floor. It crossed my mind that perhaps I should be paying more attention to her but she seemed quite content putting shapes in holes, then tipping them out again.

Picking up a guidebook for the area I learnt a little more about Kasanka National Park. The park was run by a charitable trust, formed in the mid-1980s when a visitor to the area heard shooting and thus concluded that if there was poaching, there must be animals. He resolved to save the place from total depletion and, more than a decade later, herds of animals that had nearly been wiped out from the area were now thoroughly re-established and thriving.

"Stephen," I said, looking up from my reading, "we're in quite a place here!"

"Yeah?" He acknowledged my interruption before returning to the matter at hand. "Try it the other way up, Matthew."

"We need to look out for the sitatunga," I carried on blithely. "It's an antelope – really quite rare. This is one of the few places in Zambia, let alone the world, where you can see one. Indeed, if you're lucky, you can spot herds of them during the mating season although they are normally solitary animals."

"OK," he said. "Anything else we should look out for?"

"There's abundant bird life."

"Not with our two children around!"

"Well, no, they don't really help! But it seems that there are a lot of rare birds here that you may never see again: over 330 species have been recorded including such rarities as the Pygmy goose, Ross's loerie, osprey, the wattled crane and – oh!" I gasped and stopped.

"What is it?" Stephen looked up, concerned by my tone of voice.

"Pel's fishing owl." I completed the list and looked over at Stephen. "It seems our sighting yesterday was a bit more impressive than we gave it credit."

He smiled, further comment interrupted by, "Dad, where does this bit go?" from Matthew.

"Talking of rare sights, we've been advised to go to see the bats sooner rather than later."

The straw-coloured fruit bats are unique to Kasanka National Park and the primary reason for us choosing to go there over Christmas. During November and

December they migrate en masse – over five million of them every year, the largest aggregation of mammals in Africa. The reasons for migration to Kasanka are clear. Here they find plentiful fruit: wild loquat, water berry and red milkwood, all ripe at the same time. They choose to roost in the Mushitu Forest, an area of no more than 2.5 acres, yet as they are large bats, with a wingspan of up to 85 centimetres, their living space is cramped. They hang from every available branch and even from one another. Each evening they leave the forest to search for food, returning to sleep through the day.

What wasn't understood was why they left, nor where they went. Given there are millions of them it would be reasonable to assume there were other sightings of significant sized migrations and groupings around the world. I wondered if perhaps they spent ten months of the year on holiday in the Congo, in the middle of a rainforest where no human had ever been (or at least no human with access to the internet).

"Can we make it tonight?" I asked.

"What time was recommended?"

"They leave their roosts just before sunset, so we're best being there a little early – about 17.30. How are we going to deal with these two? We're not supposed to make any noise, if at all possible."

Eleanor hit the blocks with her hammer and yelped with delight. Matthew slotted the final piece into the jigsaw, grinned and then broke it all up again. Stephen stretched and turned his full attention to me. "I guess it's best if you and your father go tonight, and then perhaps I will go tomorrow evening. We've got several days here yet, so plenty of chances to see them."

"OK – if you're sure."

"Yes, that's fine. Wait and see. I'll have the children fed and bathed and ready for bed before you get back!"

In the shade of the mulberry tree

We pulled up at the foot of the Fibwe Hide and were greeted by a scout employed by the park. He told us we had to be quiet and led us through a small piece of woodland to a clearing.

"That is the forest," he explained. "They roost in there. At night they search for food." He glanced at his watch. "They will be coming soon."

We waited patiently, whispering to pass the time. It was cooler as the sun set and we had no seats. Then, gradually, a few bats emerged and flew into the sky. The scout pointed them out: I felt foolish, given I just assumed they were birds. "They are slow tonight," he said.

There were just one or two…then a small group flew out…then more and more. Soon the air was filled with bats, high above, merging with the setting sun and the greying sky. It was mesmerising: the sound of hundreds of wings flapping, the chattering as they prepared for takeoff, their bodies covering the heavens. Then all of a sudden the display was over as they disappeared behind us. We couldn't quite believe that was it, that twenty minutes had truly passed.

The scout shook his head. "They are leaving," he said and turned to guide us back to the car.

∼

Their annual disappearance remained a mystery but sadly Stephen got the raw deal. The next night he went and was disappointed by the display, just a few bats emerging from the forest. The following morning we were taken on a walking tour to the woods, to climb up into the trees to see the bats roost, but they were gone. A week ago there were millions of bats hanging from the sturdy trees. We could only look through the maze of empty branches and imagine what an incredible sight it must have been.

LAZY DAYS

My father and I returned to the Fibwe Hide. This was an amazing construction, set high up in a giant mululu tree. From the foot I could see a ladder that appeared to go on forever. Reaching the top of this we discovered that it was not the end: there followed a series of smaller steps and platforms meandering around the branches up to a final sizable viewing platform, about 18 metres above ground.

    We arrived out of breath, but the climb was worth the effort. The view over the Kapabi Swamp was astonishing. The sun was already beating down and we could make out pools of water from its shimmering light. In the middle distance was woodland, more of the miombo forest that covers Zambia. To our right and behind us was the empty bat forest, a dark verdant mass. We struggled to make out any animals, even with

Lazy days

our binoculars, as the reeds covering the swampland hid creatures too well. It was the wrong time of day for them anyway. We knew early morning or evening was better for animal viewing but with my children neither time was easy to accommodate.

Regretfully we turned to leave. I glanced down through the branches, platforms and ladders. Suddenly, fear gripped me. It was a long way down, a very long way down. I looked back at Dad. He was in his seventies and instinctively I felt very protective of him. I couldn't allow him to go first: it had to be me. However, the thought of trusting myself to let even one foot go down the next step, to be sure I'd keep hold of the ladder, petrified me.

You've got to do it, I told myself. There's no other way. It's hardly as if the fire brigade can come and rescue you.

Cautiously I turned around and grasped whatever sturdy wooden banisters I could find. *You got up safely. It is secure. There is no reason to panic.*

The first few levels were fine. The final ladder, a pretty much vertiginous drop of maybe ten metres, made me catch my breath again. *One step at a time,* my mind repeated as a mantra, *one step at a time.*

Right foot, left foot to join it, arm, arm. Right foot, left foot to join it, arm, arm. Each rung was slowly negotiated. Halfway down my right leg began to ache. I realised that swapping to left foot first would ease the strain but my routine was set, my confidence came from the rhythm and pattern.

By the time I reached the bottom I was aching all over from the tension of the descent. I looked up at Dad, following carefully behind me.

"Oh!" he said. "That was hard work! What an amazing view – do you want to run back up to take another photo?"

I stared at him. He winked. I groaned and we returned to camp.

※

Another lazy afternoon was spent on the veranda of the main building. It was beautifully set out with a panoramic vista over the lake. A couple of large tables were available, but best were the deckchairs arched around the view. We could all sit back, read books, enjoy the landscape. Everything was quiet: the comforting noise from a few pots and pans and the idle chatter of the workers emerged from behind the building while we appreciated the raw beauty of wild nature laid out before us. The thatched roof overhead protected us from the drizzling rain that descended just after lunch. Even the children seemed to respect the quiet.

In the morning we had had a walking safari around the lake. A maid at the Lodge watched over Eleanor but Matthew came with us. We had hoped to see the elusive sitatunga antelope, but our closest brush with wildlife was walking over the skin of a python. It didn't look that old, still retaining its colour and markings. I had tightened my hold on Matthew's hand.

At the mid-point of our walk we paused to look back across the lake to the huts lining the shore: virtually unnoticeable, as if they had grown up with the trees and reeds. The main building merged into the landscape, like a wooden rugby ball topped by thatch that mirrored the thriving reeds in the marshland before us.

Away to one side the route was muddy. We were shown the footmarks of hippos, left as they trekked across the ground in their nightly forage for food. These were old, dehydrated markings from the end of the dry season. Their nocturnal forays now were closer to the river, on higher ground where their footing was more secure.

The guide also showed us a big mud basin. "This is where the elephant comes. We get visited occasionally by a bull elephant. Maybe you will see him as his comes to cool off and roll in the mud." From then on I kept glancing at the trees, expecting him to emerge at any point, but thinking that he would not be impressed to find us in his favourite spot. I charged Matthew with the job of spotting him. He had long since given up on walking and was being passed between the men.

From my seat on the veranda I scanned the horizon, recollecting the path that we had taken. There was nothing before me but waving grass, a few birds in flight overhead. Behind me, the guide came onto the veranda. His boots knocked sharply against the floor, but his appearance was neither disruptive nor unwelcome. Like everyone, he first stopped to take in the view, to breathe in the fresh air, to listen to the chattering of the crickets and birds.

"Madam, see, a sitatunga," he said, pointing over to the far side.

Stephen and I immediately sat up and took notice. We could see nothing. We scoured the reeds, looking for some sign of a difference in colour, some movement or sign of life. All we saw was a golden brown feather of papyrus, stretching out across the lake.

Slowly, carefully, he explained what he had found – and there it was, as clear as day. I could see the curved horns above the reeds, the inquisitive face looking around, alert for any potential danger. Through binoculars the identity was confirmed by the white splodges on the ginger head and the hint of stripes across its back. He was partially hidden, so no chance of seeing the hoofed feet specially adapted for inhabiting the swampy marshland. Satisfied that no predator lurked in the grasses the solitary male bent his head to resume eating.

※

Despite our best intentions to refill with fuel, our lazy schedule and low levels of diesel in The Bishop meant that an argument was brewing. Driving in four-wheel drive and using the air-conditioning burned diesel faster than normal and our late night dash when we arrived at Luwombwa Lodge had cost us dear. It was Christmas Eve and there were conflicting opinions.

"I'd really like to see 'The Africa House'," I said, recalling the magic of reading Christina Lamb's book. "It's just up the road past Mpika. Ooh – and the guidebook says that Livingstone died near here – another landmark site."

"But we only have one day," Stephen reminded me. "We can't do everything. How far are they?"

"Livingstone is about half an hour, or so?"

"Or so, I'd imagine. Much longer knowing our luck. What is there to see there?"

"There's a monument where he died. Well, where the site of the tree that was planted on the spot where they buried his heart after he died. The tree, like the rest of his body, is now in London, at the Royal Geological Society. Funny that. You'd think they'd be in Westminster Abbey or somewhere similar."

"There aren't many trees buried in Westminster Abbey," Stephen commented wryly. I gave him a look. "Anything else there? I have no need to visit just to worship Livingstone's memory or trace his footsteps across Africa," Stephen continued.

"We might be able to meet the Chief."

"Hmm…Still sounds a long way for a short amount of pleasure. It's hardly going to entertain the children for hours."

I had to agree with that. Car journey, look at concrete plinth, return car journey. It would hardly expand their education.

"I guess Shiwa Ng'andu's out too," I said regretfully, having measured its distance on the map. "It is a very long way. We'd have to go back to Serenje in order to get more diesel and even then couldn't guarantee getting back. It would be better as an overnight stay, or at least en route further north." I sighed with disappointment and frustration.

"I'm sorry, I know you'd like to go," Stephen said gently, but the silence could not take hold as he set out the positive spin. "It will have to be part of our six-week tour before leaving Zambia. We can include it as part of the itinerary that tours jaw-dropping waterfalls, Lake Tanganyika and the Bangweulu Wetlands, all of which we are also not going to reach this holiday."

"You know I'm going to hold you to this, don't you?" I said, looking at him sternly over the guidebook. "It's a bizarre piece of England in the middle of Africa, red bricks and all."

He smiled. "I know. But it is just impractical."

I understood, but that was only a small consolation. I'd wanted to see Shiwa ever since reading Christina Lamb's book and it felt tragic to be so near, and yet so far. A twelve-hour drive from Lusaka with two toddlers in the car was hardly going to be repeated at the drop of a hat.

"One of the waterfalls is quite close by," Dad chipped in. He enunciated slowly and carefully, "Kun-da-li-la," and looked up from the leaflet he was reading. "The photos are stunning."

"How far is it?"

"Perhaps an hour's drive away."
I looked at Stephen. "Sound good?"
"Great!"
The decision was made. We packed up the kids, packed up a picnic and set off.

❧

After nearly a week in the park it was liberating to venture back on to the tarmac, speeding along the straight roads. We were delighted to see that there was a legible sign for the turning off: *Kundalila Falls National Monument*. Given I had spent much of my time in Zambia hunting for signs and clear directions such clarity was a welcome surprise.

I'd got my speed up and we bounced along the dirt road at some pace.

"Slow down!" cautioned Stephen.

"But we've been told that there is no great benefit to slow driving over washer-board road," I countered.

"Yes but–" there was a big jolt as we hit one of the potholes, "unexpected events can cause damage?"

I'd already slowed down. It appeared this was not the place to resume my rally driving training.

We passed a few villages, mud huts with straw roofs around a dusty communal area. Chickens pecked at the dirt, children ran along, waving at the mzungu driving past. Matthew waved back cheerily. One village opened out close to the road with the focal feature of a large pump between us and the dwellings. Women were there, filling their yellow plastic water carriers, chatting with one another. I felt quite guilty as The Bishop sprayed dust everywhere as I drove past.

The track worsened and we passed an idle grading machine. Finally the road opened out by some heaps of gravel. There was a sign indicating a price for visiting the Falls, but nobody was there to take any money. I pulled up under a thorny bush masquerading as a tree and surveyed the landscape.

There was no sign of a waterfall. Getting out of the car we heard nothing but the general noise of the bush. It was peaceful and quiet, not a soul around. None of this was encouraging.

"Where now?" I asked.

Stephen had already put Eleanor in the backpack and was investigating on the far side of the car park.

"Let's try here," he called, pointing through the grass, and disappeared.

✑

My father, Matthew and I followed more cautiously, but grew in confidence as the pathway became a more certain route. And then there was the sound of rippling water, first gently, then louder and louder, until we came upon a babbling brook.

I stopped and stared. "Is this it?" I asked, enchanted but disappointed. I was expecting something that dropped a great height, but perhaps Kundalila was just a collection of smaller waterfalls. My thoughts were lost as we saw Stephen and Eleanor further ahead.

There was a plank of wood for a bridge across the stream, then the path carried on. Through the grasses we went, surrounded by ever larger trees until at last we came out from the bush to the sound of thundering water, crashing down over sixty metres from our vantage point on the edge of the Muchinga Escarpment to a pool below.

"Ah – this is it," I exclaimed, to the amusement of my father and husband.

Instinctively I grabbed Matthew by the hand. I'd heard that someone had fallen from the top of this waterfall and come back with nothing more than a broken arm, but I wasn't about to let my son repeat the experiment. Eleanor giggled from the safety of Stephen's backpack.

Upstream there was a small bridge, far sturdier and better established than the plank we had just crossed. On the other side we followed the path down and round. The water cascaded continuously, spraying up from the splash pool below, mists sustaining the plant life all around. I paused to admire the view. Despite the crashing water the place was tranquil, filled with butterflies and, no doubt, many creatures in the growth around our feet. The name 'Kundalila' means 'cooing doves', although the water does not sound like that. I wondered if some of the birdsong I heard actually did come from doves, but was too ignorant to know.

Returning to the car we decided to have our picnic under a tree near the pathway. After checking the ground for snakes, termites or any animal droppings, we set out our blanket and sat down. Eleanor crawled all over it, but Matthew stood to eat watermelon like a Richard Scarry character.

Just as we started on the picnic an old gentleman in a worn, green cotton coat appeared from out of the bush. Clearly word had finally got round that visitors were at the waterfalls. We rose to greet him.

"Muli shani," he called to us, bustling along officiously.

"Bweno bwanji," we responded by rote in Nyanja, despite his Bemba greeting.

"Bweno, bweno," he said, nodding his head and smiling. "America?"

"No, Britain," Stephen replied. "We're living in Lusaka."

"Ah! Lusaka! Welcome, welcome. Kundalila Falls," he said, indicating their presence behind us.

Lazy days

"Yes, thank you. We have been to see them. They are amazing!" My awe at Zambia's beauty was not polite but heartfelt. Despite my anxieties about walking with a three-year-old over narrow footpaths, perilously close to a vertiginous drop, I had been smitten by the Falls. After the ferocity of the Victoria Falls they were small and delicate: one fierce jet of water, tumbling many metres into a deep, clear pool. I had refrained from swimming in it: I only half believed those who said there were no crocodiles in the river.

It was clear that Emmanuel, as he introduced himself, was actually the man in charge of taking our fee to see the Falls. It felt a little late but it was hard to begrudge the few kwacha requested. As suspicious as ever I wondered whether he really was the guardian of this heritage site, or whether he was just a local villager come to make a bit extra out of the naïve tourists. He pulled out a receipt book and I was reassured. Even in the depths of the bush, hundreds of miles from the nearest town, Zambian bureaucracy was at work.

∽

Our return was late, of course. I despaired: would we ever make a journey that didn't result in us arriving back at sunset? Stephen had driven past the main gate to the park, signing in dutifully, and now we bounced happily along through the woodland towards the lodge.

In the back of The Bishop I was planning dinner, wondering what delights the chef could cook up from our rapidly diminishing store of food. I needed to keep the best for tomorrow, for our Christmas Day feast. And we needed to eat quickly so that the children could put out their stockings for Father Christmas. This year Matthew had begun to get excited by the prospect of presents and I was looking forward to seeing his face in the morning.

Caught up in all my preparations I barely noticed when the engine cut and The Bishop rolled unexpectedly to a halt.

SAVED BY AN ANGEL

"Why've you stopped?" I called from the back seat.

"I haven't" Stephen responded.

"Well, you have! What's happened?"

"I don't know." He tried to turn the engine on, but there was nothing. Again – forlorn hope: barely a sound. The Bishop had never had a working light for the glow plugs warming up so we could not tell whether anything was getting through to them.

"I can't think what's wrong," Stephen said, scratching his chin. "We have plenty of fuel and I didn't notice anything unusual as I was driving." Stephen opened up the bonnet and got out to have a look. Dad joined him.

"What's wrong, Mum?" Matthew asked.

"Well, I don't know." I turned to see his worried little face. "Don't worry. It'll soon be sorted out."

Stephen went to rummage around in the back for a torch. The sun was low and the surrounding tall trees meant little light was reaching us. I looked anxiously into the woods but could see nothing. I passed the children some raisins.

The men came back in, shutting the doors firmly behind them. Dusk had brought mosquitoes into the wood.

"There's nothing obvious," Stephen said. "Then again, I am no expert and we have no Pajero manual so…"

He left thoughts hanging in the air.

"What do we do now?" I asked. "How far are we from the lodge?"

Stephen glanced at the milometer. "Hard to know – I didn't register what it was at the gate. What's the total – about twelve kilometres? We've probably done about seven."

"So, closer to Wasa than the gate?"

"Yeah, probably." After a pause he voiced the obvious. "Our only options are to walk, or sleep here."

I looked around our car. Eleanor was fine, snuggled up in a car seat. Matthew wouldn't take up much room, but I knew from experience what a wriggler he was. Stephen and Dad were in the front seats. Stephen would sleep through anything. Dad would sleep through nothing; besides, I couldn't believe it would be good for him at his age. This left me with the back, which was currently filled with our clutter and picnic remains. There were no blankets, and already I was aware of the cooling off after sunset. It was not an appealing thought. To top it all I had no idea what Father Christmas was going to do.

The alternative was to walk five kilometres on to the lodge – possibly a couple of hours, most of which would be in the dark. We had a couple of torches, but how long would the batteries last? And the children were tired. Matthew might manage much of it, but Eleanor would have to be carried.

Fear overwhelmed me. What were we going to do? Neither of the options was great, but we weren't going anywhere. We couldn't leave the children unaccompanied and maternal instinct kicked in: *I'm not leaving them whatever happens.*

"I'll walk on," said Dad.

"Dad, you can't."

He turned in his seat. "I can! I'm perfectly fit enough to walk up to the lodge." I was chastened by his response. "Look, time is against us. Why don't I go on ahead, quickly, unhindered by the children, and you can follow?"

It did make some sense. None of us had been sprayed against mosquitoes yet. Adding weight to Dad's argument, Matthew piped up that he wanted a wee. I clambered out with potty and boy, furtively glancing into the woods, while Dad walked ahead, alone.

It was a somewhat incongruous sight: boy, potty, African forest. Shouldn't he have been running around barefoot, fearless and unhampered by civilisation, squatting where necessary, tracking animals and friends? Yet here he was dutifully doing the clean, tidy thing – which his mother promptly poured away at the roadside and cleaned up with a baby wipe.

Meanwhile Stephen had set up the baby carrier and a nappy bag full of the necessary items for our survival: nappies, wipes, nibbles, torch. I sprayed the children thoroughly, not chancing a single mosquito bite, before doing myself and passing the canister to Stephen. The powerful aroma made the children splutter and complain, and I winced myself when it caught a small graze on my shin. There was not a lot else we could do, so we locked the car and followed after Dad.

In the shade of the mulberry tree

Even before the first bend I knew this was not going to be pleasant. Matthew was not happy with being forced to walk. Our quite muted conversation was still too noisy for wildlife, so we were unlikely to spot any antelope bounding around. I shuddered: I was not going to think about what other animals could emerge from the woodland.

Matthew's complaints were so vocal that the only option was to carry him. My back wouldn't tolerate that for more than a few yards, so he was hoisted up onto Stephen's shoulders. Eleanor was transferred to me but the device for carrying her had wheels which dug into my lower back. It's not far now, I told myself. But it was: it was a long way. Every corner was a false hope, believing we recognised it and that the lodge was just a few more steps away.

All of a sudden we heard footsteps, voices ahead.

"Grandpa!" Matthew scrambled down and rushed up to meet him. He was with two men from the lodge and their bicycles. They greeted us and Dad filled us in.

"These gentlemen are on their way home, so they will go to the gate and ask the guide to radio for help."

We retraced our steps, companionably together, but I was filled with unspeakable fear. What if they didn't? What if they forgot and just continued on home? What if the guard was asleep? What if…?

The alternative was to keep walking, through the unknown forest in the dark. It wasn't really an alternative. I had to trust, and wait.

There was foolish relief that The Bishop was still there. The irony of locking a vehicle that cannot move, left in the middle of an uninhabited forest, hadn't escaped my notice. We waved the gentlemen off on their bikes, seeking assurance again that they would speak with the guard at the gate. Climbing back into the car we could only wait.

Saved by an angel

Five minutes passed. How long did it take to cycle seven kilometres? They had hardly left at any great pace, busy chatting away to each other.

Another ten minutes. Surely they'd reached the gate by now. Where was our help? Where was the rescue vehicle?

Another ten minutes. I handed out the last of the biscuits. That was it: no more food. Matthew complained that he was hungry and I could do nothing more for him.

Ten more minutes. It was dark now. The sun had finally said goodbye to Africa and hello to – well, I supposed America was benefiting from it. The forest crowded round: darker than before, full of mysterious noises and hooting. I shivered involuntarily.

Another quarter of an hour. That was it. They'd forgotten us. They took one look and thought, *stupid mzungus. We'll teach 'em. What a laugh we'll have about this later!* We were destined to spend the night here and could only trust that someone would pass us in the morning. I would have wept with despair but the effort of keeping Matthew occupied prevented the emotions overflowing.

Another ten minutes. I-spy was very difficult in the dark.

There was a rumbling noise, then lights through the trees. What seemed an age later and a Land Rover appeared. I laughed with relief. At last we were rescued.

The manager, Edmund, had come prepared to tow us back but first he put on a head torch and bent over the engine. Stephen joined him.

"Ah, as I thought," he said. "The electrical connection has worked loose. It happens when you drive over bumpy roads. It prevents power reaching the engine so it just stops suddenly. Did you go over a bad bump just here?"

In the shade of the mulberry tree

"Not that I remember."

"Well, the turbo charger will have kept the engine going for a while. But when this connection breaks the power goes and, well, everything stops."

With a few tweaks he repaired the damage.

"Try the engine!" he called.

I turned the key. It worked!

"I'll follow you back," Edmund said, "just in case there is another problem. You were lucky to get me. The guard radioed through just before the solar power went. I was about to switch the radio off."

We explained our story – the walk, meeting the guys, waiting for rescue. He told us we were actually nearer the gate than the lodge, but I don't think he was very happy with the fact that we walked at all, particularly not my father walking alone. Given that everywhere else we went on site we had to go with a guide he had a valid point.

As promised, he followed us back to our chalet, where we parked and then staggered up to the main lodge for a much longed-for supper. "The mechanical problem and its remedy can be checked in the daylight," Stephen reassured me. An unexpected task for Christmas Day, but the evening was a time to relax, put up some stockings and hope that Santa wasn't put off by the wild animals that roamed the forest around us.

∽

I walked back to the bar area late the next night to pick up a bottle of water for our chalet. I pondered what had made this Christmas Day so unlike all the others, so unfamiliar; indeed so dissatisfying. We were away from our home and routines and I felt somewhat out of my depth.

Saved by an angel

Usually Christmas was full of excitement, anticipation: all emotions heightened by the sight of children's young, innocent faces delighting in the mystery and adventure. Christmas was all about wrapping up warm against chilly winds, lighting candles in the darkness, warm log fires burning in the grate, choirs singing well-known carols. The shopping was part of the experience, trudging down the darkened streets to find the perfect gift, wandering through brightly lit shops, sparkling with tinsel and metallic decoration. All the work beforehand, dodging in and out of the warmth to find unwanted trinkets for all the family and the battle at the supermarket to reach the tills before closing, finally came to fruition as family gather together to eat like kings, overindulging on rich food and fatty snacks, before collapsing in front of the television. The wind whistled round the house outside; inside all was warm, comforting and postprandially immovable.

This Christmas had been different. I did have family around, although somewhat diminished as Dad woke with a stomach upset and had spent most of the day in bed. And the weather had done its best to play its part: there had been drizzly rain all day. Perhaps it was simply the overpowering heat that took away much of the Christmas atmosphere? I hadn't realised just how important the cold, dark days were to my Christmas experience. Here the day had been the same length as always, varying little from the twelve hours that we had all year round.

I took in a deep breath and smelled the damp foliage, the scent of new growth. It was dry just now, although a bit wet underfoot. The onset of night had cooled the air and the humidity was not so overwhelming. All around me I heard the night noises from the park, the chatter of cicadas, the grunting from

In the shade of the mulberry tree

the hippos, the swishing of the reeds as the wind blew across the plain. I was relishing the freedom of the two-minute walk by myself and realised just how much I enjoyed being able to stretch my legs without the distraction of children. It crossed my mind that I could run away – just now – no-one would have known for ages. I could escape, run free, follow the footsteps of other emancipated women, become a bohemian artist, live off the land. Another breath and I returned to reality. I could never, ever have left them – my husband, my children. They were my life. They all enjoyed themselves today, even if the experience wasn't as I might have wished.

Despite the car disaster the previous night, we had tried to make it as Christmassy as possible for the children, putting stockings on their beds and reassuring Matthew that Father Christmas could come under the mosquito net. This morning breakfast was delayed while we opened the gifts on the veranda, still in our pyjamas. Matthew was at a good age for presents, still finding the smallest gifts exciting and an adventure. Eleanor found the whole event bamboozling, too young to open presents by herself and really not understanding what all the fuss was about.

There was no tinsel, no decoration in the lodge. I climbed the steps to the main building and greeted the workers, busy clearing away the remnants of our sumptuous Christmas dinner. I walked through to the bar to get our water. The resident chef had surpassed himself, serving up a meal of immense proportions perfectly done and perfectly timed. The chicken was just right, along with the crispy bacon, roast potatoes and broccoli – perhaps not your traditional Christmas veg but known to be eaten happily by the children. Friends of ours once told us that their holidays were now happy only if their kids were happy: I was

Saved by an angel

beginning to understand what they meant. Matthew and Eleanor enjoyed Christmas, but for me it had held nothing of the magic I recalled from my childhood and which I so desperately wished to pass on to them. Despite the amazing food and presents the day felt remarkably ordinary.

Walking back to the chalet clutching my bottle, I passed a dazzling display of small yellow butterflies, fluttering among the undergrowth. There were too many to count: a bright, cheerful presence amongst the damp green flora. How long did butterflies live for – a day? Two? All these angel-like creatures brightening up the landscape especially for Christmas Day, only to fade away, like so many of the fancy trimmings we were used to in the West.

The analogy with angels made me realise what I was missing in particular about the day: church. For as long as I could remember I had been to church on Christmas Day. As a child I showed off my presents to everyone else there, waving my legs above the pews to reveal my new luminous pink socks or delighting in someone bringing their pet hamster. As an adult I'd enjoyed the peace of midnight mass, the reassurance of familiar hymns. But today we hadn't sung any carols or read any of the traditional readings. We hadn't really acknowledged the birth of the Saviour of the World. And when all the trappings are taken away, what really matters? Tinsel and turkey, or peace on Earth?

I paused to watch the butterflies, saying a short prayer, grateful for all I had when there were so many around me who had little. I turned to look across the darkened lake to the woods beyond. Nothing was visible, the only light being from the kerosene lamps lighting my path in front of the chalets. I felt at peace again, in love with a life and a country that was offering me so much. For all my musings about the day feeling empty I recognised one thing: I didn't really miss the UK. I was with my family whom I loved and that made everything just perfect.

FIRST STEPS

Though we celebrated Matthew's third birthday in Kasanka (what idiots allow their child to be born at Christmas?), he celebrated his party on our return to Lusaka, as his school friends returned from holidays spent abroad in their home countries. It was party day, and party meant bouncy castle. And bouncy castle meant – well, straining my back, working out where to put it in a small garden that was overshadowed by a massive mulberry tree and stressing about how to return it to the hire company by ten o'clock the following morning.

"I got the small one," I stated on seeing Stephen's astonished look when he opened the back of The Bishop. "I'm hoping it will fit in the corner by the bathroom."

Together we dragged the massive tarpaulin out of the car and set it out on the ground. If the shop's measurements matched mine then there would be room.

It seemed a simple event to start with, but I now realised that children's birthday parties were immensely stressful and had decided that they shouldn't be allowed. I'd invited all the children from Matthew's class despite not knowing who most of them were. I had spent the last week ensuring we had enough food, planning what nibbles everyone would eat, how to prepare them so that they were all fresh, how to squeeze them all into the fridge and keep the flies and ants away. Or bees. I'd become anxious about bees since a swarm invaded another child's party a couple of weeks earlier, attracted to all the sweet food and, clearly, attracted to Matthew as one stung him on the leg. Those friends only lived around the corner: surely the bees wouldn't feel like eating again just yet?

My father had chosen to hide in his bedroom, away from the chaos of a dozen or more children running round. I had noticed that E-numbers were not listed on packets from South Africa or India so no doubt they would be adding to the mayhem. It was a rare moment when I appreciated that European directives could benefit the British consumer. The cake (a masterpiece by the woman at the bakery) was a lurid shade of green. It was a train, covered with sweets and candy. I just hoped that the children and parents would eat lots, or we'd be having trifle for weeks.

The castle did indeed fit where I wanted it although there was not an inch spare either side. All the extension leads we possessed were stretched out from the house across the garden to the pump that inflated the monster castle.

First steps

Matthew looked on, uncertain. He knew he wanted one, but his last experience was another friend's birthday. Matthew was bouncing away keenly when the power cut out. The castle immediately deflated and he ended up banging his back against rock-hard ground. Bees and bouncy castles: he hadn't had very good party experiences so far.

"Come on, it'll be fun!" I encouraged him. No-one was due for a couple of hours yet so we had some free time. I climbed on and began jumping. Matthew shook his head and ran back inside.

I clambered down to go to comfort him.

"Health and Safety would not be impressed by this," grumbled Stephen as I passed. He was scratching his head, staring at the leads. "The wiring on the plug on the pump looks very loose, the cables could be tripped over. Please tell everyone to stay away from this area, and we must hope it doesn't rain. Water and electricity do not mix."

I was more concerned about the far side of the inflated castle being perilously close to the wire that came down from the telegraph pole, and more immediately focused on Matthew.

"Don't worry – it'll be fine!" I exuded blasé confidence about the electrics as I rushed past.

Still, the stage was set: now all we needed were a dozen three-year-olds and their parents.

∽

After the event I collapsed into a garden chair with a cup of tea. My father emerged from his afternoon slumber, pulled up a chair and joined me with Eleanor on the rug beside us. The late afternoon sun snuck through between the mulberry tree and the wall, casting a golden glow over the toys. Somewhere in the house

In the shade of the mulberry tree

Matthew and his father were putting together the Lego set he had just received. Sherry and Precious, commandeered to do extra hours on a Saturday, had left after a steady couple of hours of washing up.

"I'm glad that's over," I said, throwing my head back and running my hands through my hair.

"I'm sure you are, love," Dad responded. "It's hard work planning all that, particularly given you had to have a back-up plan in case it rained. You've been lucky with the weather."

We looked to the sky and I had to agree. The sun had shone all afternoon, we'd moved the chairs around the garden to get the best of the shade at all times and only now were the clouds beginning to fill the sky. Tonight it would rain, but not before.

"Where's the birthday boy? Still in his birthday suit?" asked Dad.

I laughed. "Probably! He was the only one who chose to strip off completely. He's inside, putting together a Lego pirate. He opened all the presents immediately so that I haven't a clue who gave what! All I know is that they've all been very generous."

"Indeed they have," said Dad. "It was quite a mound of toys I walked past."

"And Precious and Sherry have been fabulous. I'm not sure I could have done it without them. They're just so efficient at tidying up, bringing out more food and, best of all, doing all the washing up."

"They also had time to play with the children. She's very gentle with them is Sherry, isn't she?"

"I know. She wore her 'Sunday best' too. Both she and Precious changed before the party began, so that they weren't seen wearing their uniforms." Sherry was particularly stunning in a traditional dress: glorious bright colours, not faded by the harsh tropical sun,

First steps

fitted top and full length skirt, beautifully made to complement her generous figure.

Another thought crossed my mind. "Did you notice whether they went on the bouncy castle? I secretly hope they did, but my guess is they are too couth to have a go. I remember seeing Eleanor, held by Sherry, bouncing up and down, giggling away."

In response to her name Eleanor picked up a rattle and shook it violently, frustrated that the tassel on the end didn't fall off. I laughed gently at her bemusement. She turned and beamed broadly from ear to ear, eliciting a mirror image from me. She was such a happy girl, bringing joy wherever she went. Nothing seemed to faze her much and she approached everything as if it was there to be enjoyed.

"And did you hear about Kelly's car?"

"No. What happened?"

"She reversed out of the driveway and got caught in the ditch at the side. She's been here often enough – you would have thought she'd manage to miss it. Anyway, she was in the Corolla, just an estate car, not a four-by-four, so much lower slung, and was unable to move it."

"Good heavens! What did you do?" Dad asked.

"Aah, well we do have Evans the gardener. Kelly got out of the car and we were staring at it, discussing what on earth we should do when he walked up, took one look at the situation then bent down, lifted up the back of the car and put it back down on the road."

Eleanor crawled over and pulled herself up, frustrating rattle still in her hand.

"Hello," I grinned at her. The smile was returned with a giggle. Tentatively she held my knee with one hand, removing the other to wave the toy. The noise was clearly satisfying and she looked to Grandpa for a response.

"Ooh! What a lovely noise, Eleanor," he enthused, on cue. There was more mutual smiling and beaming. "Can I have a go?"

She glanced back at me uncertainly.

"Go on," I said. "It's OK."

She turned back and held the rattle out. It didn't quite reach Grandpa. Hesitantly, cautiously she stepped towards his open arms, steadying herself on me, then suddenly letting go…one…two…and she was caught by my dad.

"Well done Ellie," we exclaimed, leaping up in joy. "Well done, indeed!"

She looked a bit baffled by our excitement, whisked up to the sky by her proud mother. But her confusion was quickly replaced by smiles and giggles as she knew something great had happened and wanted to share our pleasure with us.

And my father was almost hopping with joy at having seen his granddaughter's first tentative steps before he flew home in the morning and I returned to work.

THE COLOUR ORANGE

The guesthouse dining room almost glowed, with its sunny yellow walls, floral plastic tablecloths and bright silk flowers. I felt I was caught in an orange ball. The flickering central bulb and fan fixed the room with a golden light highlighting the typical Zambian décor.

Richie, Joan and I were waiting on our evening meal – for Joan, kapenta and nshima; for Richie, chicken and nshima; for me, an egg roll. This was my standard vegetarian travelling diet, although I had snuck a few biscuits into my suitcase in case of disaster. The service was slow and laborious but I had long since learnt the art of patience. It would come. It would be fine. It was just best not to have any deadlines.

After an exhausting day on the road, my only deadline now was bed. We had travelled on a business trip to Gwembe, but this was no businessman's jolly. A combination of tight funds and regional poverty meant that we packed everything that a small rural farming community could need from the big city into the double cab, collecting sacks for grain en route. We also picked up some locals hitching a lift to the village who rode in the open-air carriage (the back of the pick-up), bouncing along with the jumbled goods.

Richie and Joan had come to see how some of their current aid projects were progressing. I was here to see what the money actually did. I found it much easier to understand expense sheets placed in front of me if I could visualise the work that was going on. Similarly, it was easier to justify requests for additional funding from donors when I had an appreciation of what was going on at ground level.

The projects were scattered across villages and smallholdings in the Gwembe Valley. The community had developed since the completion of the Kariba Dam, which flooded a vast area of land. Just the other side of the mountains was Lake Kariba itself and their former homes. In 1960-61 'Operation Noah' supported the rescue of thousands of animals from the encroaching flood waters; their human relations were left to fend for themselves. It destroyed the Tonga people's fertile soil and along with it centuries of history and tradition. Eventually the Gwembe-Tonga organisation was set up to support their rehabilitation but little of the funding trickled down to the people on the ground. Over forty years later the people were still struggling to support themselves at this higher altitude and on unproductive earth, feeling abandoned and disrespected by the authorities. They were refugees in their own land.

A local worker was our guide. Having paid our respects to the mayor and village elders, he took us into the fields to see the results of the agricultural training

The colour orange

the locals had received. Stepping carefully between the seedlings, we met with a grandmother, tending her fields in order to provide food for her grandchildren. She was responsible for them since their parents had died of AIDS. Although probably only in her fifties she looked much older, her thin face elongated by the sagging skin, bringing down her aged cheeks. She was wrinkled: deep crow's feet surrounding her eyes, folds of empty skin bagging up under her chin. Her clothes were worn, tattered and held together by the ever-present chitenge, all thin and faded by the harsh tropical sun. Her smile revealed several missing teeth, as she bobbed a curtsy and clapped her cupped hands gently together, the standard form of deferential greeting.

Her conversation was entirely in Tonga with our guide. I waited patiently for a translation. She explained how helpful the project support had been, teaching her about crop rotation, encouraging her to plant crops other than maize for variety and income. She clearly worked very hard in hot, arid conditions: backbreaking work tilling rocky soil, constantly bending, crouching, standing, stooping. She proudly showed how she was using the Conservation Farming technique: planting in 'wells' or small round dips in the land, rather than furrows. In each well was placed three seeds, almost ensuring that a plant would grow there. Creating bowls in the earth meant that the water could collect there, not spill over into the un-planted land surrounding it and thus the maximum amount possible reached the seedlings themselves. This method was devised to make best use of the scarce water resources and highest yield from the costly purchase of seeds. Every simple step to maximise the harvest and minimise the loss was saving lives.

Showing us around her small patch of land we saw groundnuts, soya and sorghum, all of which should make good money in the market. The farmers worked together as a co-operative so, despite her smallholding, together with her friends and colleagues she could get a good price for her produce. Later in the afternoon I saw the results of this community work, as sacks of grain were being put into a purpose-built store, providing food for the year ahead. Importantly the store was clean, dry and well-ordered, minimising the risk of loss from damp, rats or theft.

"Still no rain," said Joan, as our dinner was brought by the waitress. An odd assortment of cutlery was placed on the table.

"Are they very worried?" I asked.

Joan shook her head despondently, scooping up a kapenta in a ball of nshima with her fingers. "There has been no rain for three weeks," she said. "The crops will struggle to survive."

"The drought two years ago is fresh in their minds," Richie added. "They fear a repeat. The drought not only kills the crops but also leaves the soil to burn in the sun. You saw this afternoon the rogue maize plants down by the river."

It was more of a stream, a trickle of water bending its way through a valley that our project vehicle had been able to cross without a bridge. Along the sandy shores there were clumps of maize plants pointing to the sun, their distinctive dark green leaves climbing skywards in amongst the grassy scrub and red earth. These were the side effects of the floods that followed the drought, washing away the crops in their loose soil and depositing them downstream, along the riverbed.

"The government says there isn't a drought," I commented, and I got the derisive look I expected from Joan.

"Yes, officially there isn't – yet," she said. "But in some localised areas there is no rain. There are no crops. The land is dry and barren." She banged her finger hard onto the table to emphasise each point. "What the government says, what the statistics show doesn't matter to them. They are facing starvation. No crops mean no harvest, and no harvest means no food for the next twelve months."

Finishing my Coke, I contemplated the difference between the city and rural life. In the city there was a struggle for employment, but in the country subsistence farming meant daily labour to supply enough to eat. In our travels Joan had pointed out to me the residence of a local pastor. It was a small concrete structure no more than one tiny room in size, with a flimsy roof, the outside plastering all chipped and worn.

"He is funded solely by the giving of his church members, here, in this village and district." She shook her head. "You can see: they have nothing, there is nothing to spare, yet he is to be reliant on his flock. Meanwhile, in Lusaka, they are building a brand new centre, filming for television and the pastors…"

She let the sentence hang, but it was clear that church funding was spent like all the rest. The city was rich; the villages were poor. The excuse was that pastors were to see their work as vocation, not career, and that God would provide. How galling it must have been for these educated men to scrape together the money to travel to the capital for national conventions and see their colleagues living in comparative luxury. Here the pastor had not only to minister to his congregation spread out over the countryside, where the only transport was foot or bicycle, but also to grow his own food, subject to the same vagaries of weather and nature as his fellow villagers. No wonder rural folk sought the city for training or overseas for education: the reality at home was tough.

"So, where to tomorrow?" I asked, wiping my hands and mouth on the paper serviette. Joan was looking at the ice creams.

"A new cattle dip, the school project and perhaps the orange people," said Richie.

"Orange people?"

"You'll see what I mean," he said enigmatically.

I was intrigued, but could get no more out of either of them.

∽

Joan and I were sharing a room. It had a double bed and a single beside it, looking out through a netting window. There was an en suite toilet, where Joan retreated to express breast milk while I changed. Hearing the liquid gush out and run down the drain I wondered how my children survived their early months at all. Even at my most leaky I couldn't have done that. Being a 'traditionally-built' African woman did have its advantages.

Our night together revealed more of our cultural differences. Joan needed the windows open; I was prepared to tolerate heat to avoid mosquitoes. I got the double bed, not out of any ranking but because it was the only one with a mosquito net. Stephen had allowed me on this trip with strict instructions to use a net, use coils and spray everything to prevent mosquito bites. Joan had the bed by the TV, which she watched avidly until late into the night. I suggested burning mosquito coils; she looked at me like I was from a different planet. I fell asleep tense and on edge, willing the glaring rips in the mosquito net to close up of their own accord.

∽

The colour orange

We had another early start to get most of our work done in the coolest part of the day. Richie did all the driving and Joan most of the talking when we were with the locals. I visited the community dip tank for cattle, designed to filter the herd in solitary file through a chemical bath. Cattle were a valuable commodity, not just a source of income and food but also a measure of status and wealth. I was told that the dipping would help keep them healthy across the community, minimising the spread of disease.

Nearer the houses I saw new goat accommodation that a project had funded: two storeys in a round, wooden structure with a beautifully thatched roof. The goats got the penthouse suite; their droppings, and the free-range chickens, got the servants' quarters underneath. The raising of their living quarters reduced the risk of disease, particularly during the wet season when muddy ground could cause infection to spread rapidly. I was told the wooden lattice floor was no problem to them and their droppings could be collected later and used to fertilise the soil for crops.

Late morning I was taken cross-country to visit one of the project's co-ordinators in his home. Our guide found tracks to drive on that were little more than footpaths and I was most grateful that Richie was at the wheel. As we progressed diagonally across a field (I worried about the crops) three young girls were pointed out to me, chattering to each other as they walked.

"Orange albinos," our host said. And it was true. Even from a distance away I could see they had the facial features of a person with albinism and distinctly orange skin.

Astonished, I asked if they were all one family.

"Yes," came the reply. Albinism was a rare sight, but not unheard of. In a black community the stark white skin stood out. Traditionally it was seen as a sign of witchcraft, a curse upon the family and many were murdered at birth. Alternatively the albinos were killed for their 'magical properties': the witch doctor would use their bodies to create potions promising longevity. There were also stories of babies being killed to protect the mother's reputation, as she might have been 'messing about with the local missionaries', a midwife's misunderstanding of the baby in front of her. However, orange albinism was not something I had ever heard of before. I wondered whether Stephen had ever come across it in the course of his work.

Reaching the project co-ordinator's home I – the mzungu, the honoured guest – was given the seat in the comfy chair: a moth-eaten burgundy rayon sofa whose cushion was flat and springs broken. As we settled down and Joan chatted with the family, I looked round at the humble abode, watching the chickens peck their way in through the door before being shooed out.

Our guide turned to me.

"Please, can you pray for us?"

My heart missed a beat. What do I say? My hosts had divided their one-room house by hanging plastic sacks from the ceiling and completing the internal wall with their dried food produce in sacks beneath. They were reliant on the produce of a small patch of land outside the draughty door to feed them for a year. They had no spare clothes, all water came from the river and the only route to the village was by foot. I had everything I could ever need and more: I had health insurance, I comfortably paid for education, I had a four-wheel drive to get me around town, I could afford flights home.

I mumbled something about God's providence and grace; but knew that I had no right to speak there.

✺

The colour orange

The journey home to Lusaka was uneventful, but I was quiet, absorbing all I had seen in little more than twenty-four hours. Gwembe had shown me real poverty, how people fought to survive on a daily basis. I saw mud huts, poorly thatched smoky rooms home to families of children. I saw expanses of dusty ground, unable to be irrigated, wasted due to the nomadic harvesting of crops. I saw the results of massive flooding, as the swollen river had swept away a bridge, ravaged the local farmland and cut itself a new path across the valley floor. I saw chickens wandering into the houses, free-ranging through gaps where there should have been doors but which instead were covered with sacking or plastic.

I listened to tales of hope, never despair. For despite the lack of luxury, the constant effort to grow food and survive, the battle against the elements as the weather chose to be unpredictable, not one person I met was anything other than cheerful, welcoming and generous to a fault. *This year the rains will be good. This year the harvest will be plentiful. This year is a year of hope.*

As the concrete high rises of the capital city came into view all I could picture was the grandmother in her field, weather-worn and ragged, creased and wrinkly, but standing tall against the pure blue sky, smiling, proud that she was providing for her family and expecting better this year.

AFRICA'S WINNING

"Ellie, how do you manage it?"

I grabbed a wipe and scrubbed her hands clean, again. We were having a lazy Saturday morning with a chocolate treat at the bakery. Matthew was eagerly munching his half of a *pain au chocolat*: no-one else was going to get a look in. Eleanor was spreading hers all over herself, the pram and anything else within range. She smiled winningly through her chocolate-smeared face.

Despairing I returned to the paper. The previous day had been Budget Day. As an accountant I felt obliged to pay some attention to this. A few days earlier I had met someone from the UK who was working as an advisor to the Department of Finance and had said that his main aim was to get the budget out before he left. In fairness, the budget was presented to Parliament only a week late, thus hinting at some level of organisation, plan and intention within the Treasury department.

The papers were full of anger at the proposals. Some were calling for calm; some were calling for mass protest and action. *The Times* and *The Daily Mail* were largely government-controlled so their reportage of the budget was favourable. *The Post* was a little more balanced and all three printed the Finance Minister's speech verbatim.

The furore was because the government had introduced two new higher tax rates for those earning over K980,000 (approximately £130 per month). They'd also raised the minimum level for paying tax, nearly doubling it, but that benefit was lost in the vitriol about the top tax bracket. It was a complex situation. The majority of people in the country didn't actually earn as much as the minimum level (about £30 per month) but then the majority also didn't declare their earnings, whether they were liable to tax or not. Incremental rates of 35% and 40% were punitive for salaries that barely provided a basic standard of living.

Even with this increased governmental income there was a freeze on public servant's wages. The capital expenditure required for new roads, schools, healthcare facilities, dams or irrigation was all budgeted to be funded by donor aid. Thankfully there was to be increased expenditure on security, so at least we'd all be safe.

"Hello Daddy!" called Matthew.

"Hi there!"

I put down the paper and turned to my husband. "What can I get you?"

"Just a coffee, thanks."

"Cwassant!" said Matthew, eagerly. Eleanor threw hers on the floor. I growled, and went to the counter to place another order.

In the shade of the mulberry tree

"How was Andrew?" I asked Stephen on my return. His late arrival was because his supervisor had called from the UK. The whole phone call was going to be easier without his children crawling around so (ever grateful for an excuse) we'd escaped to the bakery.

"Fine, encouraging as ever. He's planning a visit in a couple of months' time."

"Oh, that'll be nice. Did he offer any particular advice?"

"Largely just to keep going. It's hard to pinpoint what he says that is so encouraging. I guess he's seen it all before, he knows how difficult it can be to get things through the system, he's not at all fazed by the reagents still being at the airport, that sort of thing."

"Even though its twenty-eight degrees outside and they should be kept refrigerated?"

"Yep, somehow it will all be fine," Stephen smiled. "I told him about the weather – still no sign of rain. How long since we last had a downpour?"

"At least two weeks," I said. "They're getting very worried at work."

"Well, I asked Andrew to pray about it. Meanwhile, the rest of the day is mine! What are the plans?" He rubbed his hands together in gleeful anticipation.

"Plans? Plans? We're in Africa – you think I've got plans?"

Stephen laughed at my incredulity. "I see you've finally settled in then!"

I laughed too. "Yes. I hate to admit it but really we're all doing very well."

The waitress arrived with the coffee and croissant. Matthew's eyes sparkled with delight. Stephen sat back to enjoy his coffee. Matthew grabbed his book and came to sit next to me. We looked at the pictures of a family, learning the simple associated words.

Africa's winning

"Mummy, Daddy, boy," he said dutifully, pointing at the pictures.

"That's right," I said. "That boy is their child. Tell me, who is my child?"

"Matthew!" he beamed.

"And who else is Mummy's child?"

"Eleanor!" he declared. We were on a roll and my mathematical instincts took over.

"So how many children does Mummy have?"

"Two!" came the reply, sharp as a button.

"Impressive," mumbled Stephen from behind his latte.

"And how many children does Daddy have?"

"Ten! One, two, three, four, five, six, seven, eight, nine, ten!" Matthew counted.

I looked at him, I looked at Stephen.

"I think you've got some explaining to do!"

∽

Andrew's prayer clearly worked. The next day there was torrential rain. I made a mental note to pass more prayer requests Andrew's way, while Stephen dropped into the laboratory to check on some experiments he'd left running.

"You're late back," I exclaimed when at last he reappeared.

"I know," he said wearily. He took off his T-shirt, soaking wet just from dashing to and from the car. "Give me a moment to change and I'll explain."

I took a Mosi from the fridge, instinct telling me this was the sort of sustenance he needed. While Matthew, Eleanor and I did some scribbling on the table (some of it on paper first), Stephen talked.

"They've installed new air-conditioners all over the lab. Now, you would think that was a good thing. Well, I

In the shade of the mulberry tree

suppose in many ways it is, and certainly the management have welcomed this gift." He stretched his legs out in front of him as he leant back on the sofa. "Unfortunately, they don't work. Well, they work as in they cool the air – tick that box – but they don't work in the sense that they keep blowing a fuse or burning the socket."

He took a swig of his drink. "On Friday night one of them shorted, tripping the switch. No-one seems to have noticed the beeping freezer yesterday – I can't believe there was no-one in at all, all day. So I arrive today and the first thing I hear is the beeping, the alarm going off because the freezer is warming up." Stephen hit the sofa with frustration. "Why? Why? Why? Why didn't anyone do anything? I did what I would have thought any sensible person would do: disconnect the air-conditioner and switch the freezer back on."

"What was in there?"

"All my cells. All my samples. Looks like I may have lost six months' work."

He ended despondently, staring at his bottle of beer as if it could solve the problem.

"Why are we here?" he asked, his voice flat and dull. "Just what is the point? I utterly despair!"

I looked at him, worn out, collapsed on the sofa. I loved him. We were here because of him, because of his work, because of his love for these children and a desire to provide better healthcare for them. His despondency was so unnatural, practically unheard of.

I left Matthew to his drawings and sat down next to my husband. He looked at me, great sadness in his eyes, and drew me into a hug.

"It makes me so cross!" he continued. "It is all such a waste of money, of resources, of people's lives. Last week I presented data to the lab to show them how they could save $25,000 a year. $25,000! You would think they'd be jumping at the chance! But no, the presentation just passed them by. No-one came to speak to me afterwards, no initiative to save money. Why save, when you are doing just nicely as you are?"

I could feel the anger in his tense body, frustration spat out with every word.

"Don't worry," I practically whispered. They were merely words of comfort, for I knew his anxiety could not evaporate in an instant. "We're in Africa. There is always a solution."

He kissed my head and then I looked up and kissed him, a long deep kiss full of love and promises.

"It'll be fine. You know that, don't you?"

"Yes," he sighed. "We're in Africa."

WRITING HOME

I was writing an email. Conscience had been pricked and I felt I should update the oldies about how their children and, of more interest to them, their grandchildren were getting on.

> All is well here. Eleanor keeps trying to take the odd step but walking doesn't seem to be high on her agenda yet. She just wobbles, falls down on her bottom and giggles endearingly. Then Sherry, Precious or I pick her up and give her a cuddle.

She'd never get anywhere with all this attention lavished on her. I was unable to stop myself though, as her gorgeous smile, brilliant blue eyes and beautiful blonde curls pulled my heartstrings every time.

> Matthew is progressing fine at school. He seems to have plenty of friends, some of whom are brave enough to invite him round to play. He's loving swimming and splashes madly around with his armbands on. The pool is quite pleasurable now: a cooling dip in the hot days. It is lovely to then get out and lie on the grass, drying off in the sun.
>
> My work remains pretty manic. I have been trying to persuade the heads of department to create a budget for the coming year. Obviously now, as January concludes, this is coming slightly late. It is their first attempt, so I am letting them away with it. I doubt anyone will keep to it anyway!!

Oh, such cynicism! I should have had more faith in my colleagues. They were trying really hard and were aware that future funding from donors might depend on this system being in place. Richie had made that very clear to them. Then again, he was due to leave the country soon after a final month of travelling. Selfishly, I had tried to find ways to keep him there, but his frustrations mounted, the contract ended and he had plans for a career in the UK. It looked like the battle to get a budget completed was mine alone.

Richie decided to take everyone at work tenpin bowling for his leaving do. Explaining to thirty Zambians what to do was hilarious. None of them had ever been inside a place like it; many of them never would again. The whole business of putting on the special shoes took half an hour, as the locals guessed what size feet they had again and again. Then there was a fuss over which ball to use, some of the women opting for weights I wouldn't dream of carrying, even less so swinging down a bowling alley. The basic principle wasn't so hard to grasp, although I did have to physically restrain one woman from having a practice shot down a seemingly empty alley behind her. The

In the shade of the mulberry tree

eight-year-old's birthday party might not have appreciated her fervour. At work, no-one has stopped talking about it since. Certainly Richie went out with a bang.

> Stephen works as hard as ever. His days are spent dashing from one end of the hospital to the other, from patients to lab and back again. He now has a local doctor on the team in addition to his supervisor, which takes away a lot of his worries about the day-to-day patient care. The patients seem to require a lot of work. I guess this is hardly surprising, but he battles daily with ways to keep them alive, and to keep the nurses interested in keeping them alive.

I pondered these poor children and their struggles with their health. Sometimes it all seemed so futile, like we were the only ones who cared enough to do anything.

I signed off and, grabbing my cup of tea, sat down to read the school magazine. I enjoyed this quiet moment each week when I learnt what the children had been up to – the school trips, the fundraising activities, the latest social events. I read through happily, and was interested to see that they were looking for new teachers from August for the next academic year. "Does anyone know of any international teachers who would be interested in applying?"

I thought of the teachers I knew and doubted it. Most were quite settled where they were, had family commitments and probably didn't feel they could just give it all up for a whirl in Zambia. They'd be fools not to, I thought, as it was a fantastic country to live in. Then I remembered how little I had wanted to give up my comfortable life in London and knew I couldn't blame them. How things changed: now I was utterly content and I was living in unmitigated luxury (if I ignored the bugs).

My sister: she might be an option. No children, just a husband on the way. Something told me she wouldn't do it. She had only just moved from one end of the UK to the other, so a cross-continental leap might seem too much. She probably wanted to settle down and establish herself.

What about Stephen's sister, Gwyn? What were her plans for next year? I struggled to remember our last communication, but I knew her current contract was going to end in the summer. I thought she said she was thinking of going back into teaching, finding some post in the UK. Heck! She's young, free and single – maybe she'd like a whirl in Zambia!

I returned to the computer and began typing.

Dear Gwyn,
Just thinking of you. Matthew's school is looking for teachers next year. Would you be interested in applying?

THE BISHOP FALLS APART

The Easter holidays had arrived. I couldn't believe how quickly my year was scampering through: in just a couple of months we would be flying home for a month. The rains had almost stopped and the days were once more long, sunny and dry. Everywhere was covered in lush green growth, revelling in the rain-soaked land.

We were taking the opportunity to travel out of Lusaka for a long weekend with some friends from church, this time travelling to the west. I told myself that these were valuable life experiences for my children, experiencing Africa in the wild. In reality, given they were aged three and one, the experience of African bush was primarily for Stephen and me: our memories would last longer. Gwyn was also with us, visiting for a fortnight, which had the happy

The Bishop falls apart

coincidence of being at the same time as the job interviews for school.

I had taken the advice of a magazine someone lent to me at playgroup. It had said that the road going west to Mongu was dreadful and the best route was to head north then turn left at Landless Corner.

It didn't say that from then on the dirt road was washer-board, that we'd be bouncing up and down for four hours and that the rains would have transformed whatever was good six months ago into a potholed, rock-dodging assault course.

Stephen was driving and decided that speed was the best approach. The locals were helpful, waving furiously at him to slow down. Thankfully he did, as moments later the road became two narrow tyre-width tracks, gaping holes either side and underneath the belly of The Bishop. It was unclear what was holding the remaining road together but it was obvious that 'off-road driving' at this point led to disaster.

The Bishop made a valiant attempt to traverse the road, but she, like us, was extremely grateful to reach the garage at Mumbwa. She had drunk a lot of diesel getting her air-conditioned passengers there and we still had over 100 kilometres to go to Mukambi, a lodge just off the main Lusaka-Mongu Road by the River Kafue.

"Something's wrong," Gwyn said, as we began the final stretch on decent tarmac road.

"It's a bit bouncy," I chipped in from the back.

"Boing! Boing!" demonstrated Matthew. Eleanor giggled.

We were rocking along with nothing but trust in The Bishop's suspension. We might bounce, but at least we were comfortable.

After the checkpoint at Natusanga Gate we drove with the Kafue National Park (KNP) on one side of the road and a Game Management Area (GMA) on the

In the shade of the mulberry tree

other. The difference between these two was legal: in the Park it was illegal to kill, poach or remove any habitat, in the GMA the animals also have precedence but it was controlled by locals and lodges rather than the government. We saw antelope crossing from one side to the other: they took no notice of the technical difference between the two.

We arrived after our friends, shortly before sunset, exhausted, confused and – worst of all – laughed at.

"What took you so long?" said Margriet.

"Why didn't you take the Mongu road from Lusaka?" asked Eckhard. "It has just been resurfaced."

I felt stupid for having suggested the other way; even more so when morning light revealed the real damage to The Bishop. Unloaded and unpacked there was a distinct tilt to her body, and this was made worse by a flat rear tyre. The spare was put in place and then the whole vehicle limped to the lodge workshop. Our journey home was dependent on their men fixing our damage.

୬

To my mind, this was the way one should always camp. The tents were spacious, made of quality canvas. Inside each were two single beds and bedside tables. There was even an electric light hanging from the central pole. Above the tent was a thatched awning, extending over the concreted terrace to the front, providing extra shade. Here we found a couple of chairs and a table, with a view through the bushes to the River Kafue. The only drawback to this campsite was the lack of en suite toilet and shower facilities. It wasn't like any camping I had ever done before, but a style I thought I could get used to.

We had our usual basic kit: plastic mugs, plates and bowls; Weetabix for breakfast – as always – with UHT milk; bread and cheese for lunch. I hoped they'd both remain edible for the next three days after being kept in a cool box with nothing but a couple of ice packs.

We were put to shame by our friends in the neighbouring tent. Margriet produced a tablecloth and napkins for lunch, wine glasses and a much more varied spread. We gazed in awe and admiration as the five of them quietly sat down to eat. At our tent chaos reigned with Matthew and Eleanor running around and bread doorstops (we forgot the bread knife again) being eaten awkwardly.

Dinner would be a more sedate affair as we'd planned to eat from the lodge's menu at the main buildings, a short walk downstream. These buildings were a beautiful construction. Vast beams held up a thatched roof, the apex high above our heads. Different levels made for comfortable room spaces, all opening out with a view of the river below and the park beyond. Matthew enjoyed running up and down the steps, Eleanor toddled after him while Stephen and I watched anxiously. Without the constant need to entertain small children, I could have sat there all day, drinking endless cups of tea until it became time for gin and tonic. I would have read books, flicked through magazines, enjoyed the peaceful scenery and the soothing sound of lapping water.

On the other side of the lodge was a kidney-shaped swimming pool and another small, shallow, circular pool. They were icy cold. Despite the warmth of the early afternoon my dip was brief and I soon joined Gwyn on a sun lounger, leaving Stephen in the water with the children.

"This is the life!" grinned Gwyn, settling back with her eyes closed.

In the shade of the mulberry tree

"Not bad, is it." I watched my family playing happily together. "Are you interested in a safari drive this evening?"

"Sounds good. Are we likely to see anything?"

"Well, you never know, although the end of the rainy season, with grass up to our shoulders, is not the best time to spot animals."

"Shame. Still, it will be an adventure."

"Certainly will."

Margriet and Eckhard had gone out for a drive in their vehicle but The Bishop's confinement had prevented us exploring the area. We would use the Lodge's guides for an evening drive. I'd have to make an appointment at the mechanic's as soon as I returned – assuming The Bishop would make it back to Lusaka. "When do you go into school?"

"Tuesday," Gwyn said.

"Excited? Scared?"

"Petrified!" said Gwyn with feeling.

"You've nothing to lose," I responded. "There's no reason why you shouldn't get a teaching job and I'm sure you'd enjoy it. I can't believe we've been here nearly a year now – only a month or so until we go back to the UK for four weeks."

"Time's flown by, hasn't it."

It certainly had. I couldn't believe I'd survived this year. I'd got maids, a furnished house, a car, a job, my son in pre-school, my daughter in–

"Stephen!" I shrieked.

Behind him, Eleanor had taken it upon herself to jump into the smaller pool.

The water closed over her head.

He turned round and saw the flapping arms.

In seconds he strode over, leapt in and pulled her out. She coughed, and spluttered, and cried. I ran over to them, longing to cradle my baby. How did this happen, when we were all just there, watching, chatting, idling away time? All the worries about wild animals around and I couldn't even take proper care of my daughter. All pool activity was promptly curtailed and we returned to safer ground.

∽

After a day of inactivity we decided on a night-ride. We wanted to see leopards and allegedly the KNP was full of them. It was virtually assured that we would see some big cats.

We were advised to wrap up warm and were given extra blankets by our guide. The children were fully clothed, we were all covered in mosquito repellent, the evening was warm and I wondered why it had been recommended to wear sweaters. We clambered on board the safari vehicle: a Land Cruiser with no roofing. Our driver and a spotter were seated in the front; we were on three staggered rows of seating bolted and welded to the rear. We were told to sit down and enjoy the ride. Stephen and I trapped the children between us and told them they had to be quiet. So entranced were they by the experience that they had no need to make a sound.

Before we had gone a few hundred yards we came across an elephant: a solitary male working hard at consuming a tree. He had his back to us and didn't seem too upset by the clicking cameras as we gazed on the show of strength. Our driver and guide turned off-road and round towards the back of the bushes so we could get a better view. Most amazingly, from behind we could not tell that he was there. How it was possible to hide the largest land mammal behind the small thicket of bushes and trees I could not comprehend, although I conceded the foliage was dense following

In the shade of the mulberry tree

the rainy season. From one side there was nothing but a gentle waving of branches, as if in a breeze; on the other a voracious and potentially lethal animal the size of a double-decker bus was having supper.

Our drive took us over Hook Bridge and into the park on the other side of the Kafue River. From the heights of a small outcrop we drank our sundowners, Matthew running wild for a few sacred moments, wearing off the hyperactive effects of his orange Fanta. In the distance we viewed a massive herd of buffalo grazing, a blue-grey line on the horizon surrounded by a small dust cloud.

Without the sun the air cooled rapidly. As the vehicle drove off I realised that the open-air nature of the safari vehicle allowed the wind to blow right through all the clothing. The blankets were hastily pulled up over our knees, the children were cuddled between us to keep warm.

Darkness fell but, despite valiant efforts by our guide, it was not a night for big cats. As we returned to the park gate we spotted another elephant in a small village of mud huts. Here we saw how destructive they could be, as we watched him stomp around the houses, delighting in the fruit and vegetables the people had been growing. Our driver called to the residents through their windows and they shouted back but, like during a violent storm or blinding blizzard, it was a time to batten down the hatches and stay inside where it was safe.

∽

The next day we went on a river cruise. The Kafue was one of the longest rivers in Zambia, starting in the north and meandering down to the Zambezi. We had crossed it on the pontoon last August, close to its final destination, having made its way across the flats, where it spreads out over the wide valley to create unique marshland habitat. Here, though, it was wide and graceful, arcing round the countryside, trees drooping over the edges. We were five children and five adults but the ride was beautiful, peaceful and relaxing. I got a short break from watching Eleanor as the older girls enjoyed walking up and down the boat with her.

"So, Gwyn, tell me again, what happened with your passport?" Margriet settled back into a director's chair on the large, flat deck.

"Well, I took it up to London a week before I left to get a visa from the Zambian High Commission."

"But you're British – do you need a visa?"

"No!" interrupted Stephen. "I told her you could buy them at the airport when you arrived. But I'm only her brother so…"

"You rotter," she squealed. "The information I had was that you had to have a visa on entry, so I was doing what I was told." A small grunt came from Stephen and she continued. "I'd filled out the forms and dropped them in on the Saturday. It was closed so I put it all in an envelope in a letter box on the side of the building."

"Left it!" Stephen blustered. "Left it: no receipt, no evidence of deposit. And it wasn't even necessary!"

"Look, bro, this was in London, the UK. How was I to know? Anyway, I rang up on Tuesday to ask when it would be ready, only to be told that they did not have it. I explained what I had done and they denied any knowledge of receiving the envelope. They even had the cheek to suggest that I hadn't actually delivered it!"

"Because you dreamt it, or were – how do you say in English – sleepwalking, or something?"

We all laughed at Margriet's cynically accurate interpretation.

In the shade of the mulberry tree

"Anyway, the long and the short of it is that I had to report it stolen and then had three days to get a new passport, and visa, before flying out here. I did it but – phew! It was a close-run thing!"

"What is it about your family and lost passports? Didn't you lose them too?" Margriet turned to Stephen. There was the hint of a blush.

"Yes, OK, we did," he said. "Clearly we're not safe to be let loose with important documents. Nor with credit cards, it would seem. Someone is running around Southend using mine at present. I guess the UK isn't number one on the least corrupt nation list yet, not by a long chalk."

"I think it is Finland," I said, to a sea of blank faces. "Number one on the list, that is. It was in the paper the other day."

"Where was Zambia?" Margriet asked.

"Eleventh. From the other end."

"Ach, it is terrible. Such a beautiful country, such natural wealth and minerals, such lovely, amazing people yet…" Margriet shrugged her shoulders. "Sometimes it is hard to see how such countries will ever pull themselves out of poverty. Nature is harsh for them but, as a nation, they can only work to help themselves."

A loud harrumph startled us, as a disgruntled hippo surfaced nearer the boat than either he or us would have liked. Carefully our driver slowed the engine down, steered clear and turned the boat towards home.

"Daddy, I need a wee!"

"You'll have to hold on, love."

"But I can't," Matthew whined, starting to hop up and down uncomfortably.

Stephen and I shared a despairing look.

"Back of the boat," said Eckhard, nodding to the railing and the river. There was little choice but to pee over the side. The retreating hippo eyed us uncomfortably. "Don't worry – I'm sure the locals put much worse into the river."

The driver smiled at our little boy, completely unperturbed. I had to assume Eckhard was right.

※

Back at the lodge we heard that our car had been fixed. Stephen went to fetch it and proudly drove back to the campsite.

"He says he's welded the axle back on. We probably should have it checked out when we get home."

I groaned, thinking only of the hassle of getting it to the garage, the cost of the inspection and subsequent repairs (which the mechanics would no doubt come up with regardless of the need) and how little I would trust what anyone said anyway.

For now, though, we had transport, so we loaded the car and had a smooth journey on the main road back to Lusaka. The car survived, but we returned to bad news.

HOPE, AND HOPE DASHED

The afternoon we got back from Mukambi I opened my front door to find our neighbour's maid in tears. Instinct said that it wasn't me she needed, but a friend she could relate to.

"Precious!" I called. She came running and I retreated into my bedroom, intrigued to know what was wrong.

Not much later, Precious came to speak with me.

"It is Johnny," she said. "He crashed his car last night and is in hospital."

Horrified, I asked what happened.

"He was driving back from the pub. At the top of Los Angeles," she waved her arms in the general direction, "he was turning right and a car came straight into him, at the side."

Hope, and hope dashed

I could picture the junction at the top of the hill, a turn I had often thought dangerous as it was a blind spot for seeing traffic coming up the hill towards you. I shook my head, not knowing what I could do. I did not know him well, but he always struck me as a cheerful Irishman, often residing in one of the ubiquitous Irish bars.

During the week Precious kept me updated on progress. The crash hadn't caused any long-term damage but Johnny was diagnosed with malaria. By Friday he was dead.

❦

"How was the tour of school?" I asked, pouring Gwyn a glass of wine.

"You were right, it was an interview. Thank goodness you persuaded me to dress up! They were lovely though."

"I don't know the deputy very well but she has always struck me as very sensible and down-to-earth. So," I paused, anxious to find out the answer to my question, "do you want the job?"

"Oh yes! But they're looking to employ at the international fair next month, and there's only one slot and I've no international experience, so I'm not holding out too much hope."

I grinned. "They liked you. That's a good sign. I'll tell Matthew to be particularly well-behaved next term. I'd hate it to be us that wrote you off!"

Gwyn dismissed this immediately. "I don't think Matthew will be the problem. What was it his teacher said? 'He is very good at sitting at the table and working'? He's probably the most loved three-year-old in the class!"

We clinked glasses and laughed together.

In the shade of the mulberry tree

"By the way, Matthew's named the tortoises." Tanvir was leaving and had given us her tortoises. She'd called the smaller one Houdini and so Evans had been asked to spend the day creating an escape-proof pen for our new pets. "They're called Thomas, short for ThomastheTankEngine, as he says it, and TomFum, although that one was briefly Bob the Builder."

"How do you know they're male?"

"I don't." I giggled. "I guess we'll find out in due course!"

We rocked with laughter and it was in this state, or perhaps a couple of glasses worse for wear, that Stephen found us when he came in from work.

"How was your day?" I struggled up from the sofa to get him a drink.

"Oh, fine," he said, wearily. He threw down his bag and gratefully took his glass. "Blimey, I could do with this."

"Bad day at the office, love?"

"You could say that. Well, my work was fine, in the standard state of mass confusion. I left my lab technician entering data today while I went up to the ward. I came back to find him barely started, but manfully using two fingers to type into the Excel spreadsheet." He demonstrated using his index fingers the speed of data entry. "Argh! And he has a degree!"

He collapsed onto the sofa, head thrown back, took another gulp of wine to calm the nerves, ease the tension. Gwyn and I giggled. His face fell again. "Has Precious gone?"

"Yes, about half an hour ago. Why?"

"Mutende's back in hospital. It's not looking good." He was quiet now, and all the joy of earlier vanished in an instant.

"Not in remission, then?"

"No." He shook his head. "I just wish there was something I could do."

"Hey, you know how grateful Daniel is for all you've done so far. You can't cure everyone."

"I know, but–"

"And you said yourself that her chances would be low, even back in the UK."

"Yes, but..." He sighed, ran his hands through his hair and looked miserably at the ground.

I leant over and squeezed his arm. "Don't worry – she'll be fine."

But she wasn't.

༄

Johnny died of a disease with a cure. White people tended not to die of malaria, insulated as they generally were by health insurance and fearful of the symptoms at an earlier stage. Perhaps his pickled liver was unable to cope with the drugs required to combat the malaria, but his death was a surprise.

Mutende was seven. She had a disease that required a lot of expensive drugs to be given. In the UK she may have had a bone marrow transplant to rid her system of the dreadful growth in her blood. Yes, she would have been dreadfully sick, but she would have been cared for in a place of optimism, hope and expectation. In Zambia she was faced with slow and inaccurate diagnoses, a lack of affordable drugs and the non-availability of treatment.

Johnny died on the wrong side of sixty.

Mutende died on the wrong side of the poverty line.

IN THE SHADE OF THE MULBERRY TREE

There were toys all across the garden. How did children create such carnage? I knelt down and began to throw Duplo back in my beloved baskets, my stylish scheme for hiding toddler trash. I cursed, as my knee squelched into another mulberry. There was great wisdom in using the big tarpaulin as a play area on top of the scratchy grass, but keeping it in under the tree had its downside. Everything seemed to be splattered with maroon splodges.

Contrary to all I had read about the mulberry tree, ours seemed to be perpetually fruiting. I thought about how I had grown used to it during the year, from the gloom of the early days to its welcome cooling of the house in the hot months of October and November,

In the shade of the mulberry tree

and now simply appreciating its existence during the heat of the day.

Though I wasn't sure I would ever get used to the blood-red stains from its fruit. I stood up, brushing off the dust before going inside to change my trousers. From the other side of the building I could hear my children's screams of delight in the swimming pool. Stephen counted, "One…two…three…" and then there was an almighty splash. I wondered who would tire of that game first.

For now it remained warm enough to swim, but May was drawing to a close and winter approached again. I threw my dirty clothes on top of the floral blanket (still hideous) and thought back to how cold it was when we first arrived. This year I was hoping to miss the worst of the winter weather, as – at long last – next Saturday we flew home to the UK for a month.

A month! It sounded like a lifetime of a holiday. Stephen, of course, would have to spend some time working with his supervisors in London. I planned to split my time between my father and the in-laws, throwing in a couple of friends' weddings and hopeful of a few days away as a family.

A smile spread across my face. *I'm going home!* A year away and finally – *finally* – I was going to see the UK again. I'd get to see my family, to meet my future brother-in-law, to sit in an English pub, to have a choice of cheeses, to eat prawn cocktail crisps.

On the other hand, I would also have to wear jumpers and socks all day; I would need a coat and umbrella even if it looked good in the morning; and who would wash and iron all my family's clothes? I wouldn't have Sherry or Precious – how would I survive? The more I thought about it, the more stressful the imminent holiday appeared.

In the shade of the mulberry tree

In the kitchen I set out some juice and biscuits, filling the kettle ready for a pot of tea when the family had finished their swim. The water supply in the filter was running low so a few minutes were spent filling its ten-litre capacity. As the water gently dripped through I escaped to a sunny spot in the garden to await my family's return. The late afternoon sun cast a golden glow over everything. Even the remaining plastic toys looked attractive in its warmth. I decided to leave them – for now – and enjoyed a moment's peace.

I'd survived a year! Looking back, I wondered at all that had happened in twelve short months. My fear of Africa, of Zambia, had vanished. I didn't worry about creepy crawlies nor even, for the most part, about mosquitoes. I could see that malaria was seasonal and there was little chance of catching it during the dry season. Johnny's death lingered in the mind but didn't fill me with fear, and Stephen had rarely talked of his patients coming in with malaria.

Then again, Stephen's patients were worrying about many other things. HIV/AIDS, TB, pneumonia: many diseases that would kill a malnourished child. As I caught sight of yet another mulberry falling – splat – onto the tarpaulin I bit my lip. Here I was, watching food go to waste in a country where children were starving.

The conflict between my wealth and the nation's poverty hit me again and again. I didn't feel wealthy - after all, I drove an eleven-year-old car. Then again, I always had food on the table. I had a table. No, two. Or even four, if you included the desks in the spare room. How did you calculate true wealth? Quantity of tables owned?

In the past year I had furnished an entire house from scratch. I thought that with a degree of pride, as we had arrived with virtually nothing. Of course there were still

In the shade of the mulberry tree

more things I would like to have (a coffee table, bringing my table-count to five?) but we were functionally complete. My year seemed to have a peculiar catalogue of achievements. I had cooked dinner for ten despite only having a couple of saucepans and barely enough cutlery. I had got a job – been interviewed, become a member of the local professional organisation. I had got passports stamped with employment and travel permits. I had ventured into the city centre on my own, parking The Bishop without incident.

The phone rang, breaking my reverie. I hauled myself out of the chair and out of the sunlight.

"Hello?"

It was my mother-in-law. "Would you like to speak with Stephen? He's just at the pool with the children but...yes...yes...I'll just go and– oh! He's here!"

Dripping water and traipsing towels through the dust, my family had arrived like a duck with her ducklings. They were all smiles.

"Here, let me take them," I said to Stephen. "It's your mother on the phone."

I scooped up my baby girl, planting a kiss on her cheek, and held out a hand to Matthew. "Come on, you two. Let's see if I can find some clean clothes."

❧

Ten minutes later I returned with the children, who made a beeline for the toys outside. I despaired, as their clean clothes were immediately immersed in orange-red dust and squished mulberries. I walked towards the kitchen ready to make a pot of tea, but Stephen emerged holding a bottle of wine and a pair of glasses.

"Time for a drink," he exclaimed with a grin spread across his face.

In the shade of the mulberry tree

"Careful! It's a bit early and I might not manage to cook supper," I said, but I was thinking: *Wine? From a bottle? That's mighty expensive and extravagant!*

"Oh, go on – we're celebrating."

"Celebrating? Celebrating what?"

He grinned. "You're an aunty! Ruth gave birth this morning."

"Wahoo!" I shrieked. "Go on then – get pouring!"

Outside, Stephen balanced the glasses on our old plastic table. He'd already put out the juice for the children, who were showing no interest whatsoever. They had grabbed a biscuit and run back to their toys. So much for my efforts at tidying, and the clean clothes, I thought, as Eleanor wiped chocolate-covered fingers down her trouser leg.

"There's more," he said.

"I know. Girl or boy? Name? Weight?"

He paused mid-flow. Slowly, as if scraping memories from beyond the back of his brain, he said, "Girl. Anna. Don't know the weight."

"Didn't your mother tell you?"

He shrugged and returned to pouring the wine. "Yep, but she told me it in pounds and ounces. It sounded fine and no-one seems worried, so—"

"So you instantly forgot. Typical!"

He smiled sheepishly. "But there is other news," he reminded me. "Gwyn has heard back from the school. She's got the job."

I squealed with delight. "That's fantastic! When does she start? Which year is she teaching? Is she pleased?" I gabbled.

Stephen laughed as he tried to answer all my questions at once. "August, about a week before Matthew goes back, and she's got Year 4, which she really wanted, so yes: she is pleased."

"And your mum? Is she pleased?"

In the shade of the mulberry tree

"Yes. I think an extra grandchild is partial compensation for her daughter moving overseas. Anyway, she and Dad are coming to visit around the same time so they'll be able to make sure Gwyn settles in all right."

I grabbed my wine and clinked glasses with Stephen. "Cheers!"

We sat under the mulberry tree in companionable silence, sipping our drinks. I couldn't stop thinking how fantastic my life was. My children were playing happily. My husband was home from work, from a job he loved. I was blissfully content, surrounded by beauty and the most marvellous people in the world.

"Thank you," I said softly to Stephen.

He looked at me quizzically.

"Thank you for bringing me here. I'd never have done this without you."

He smiled. He had travelled a long journey with me but did not have the character within him to gloat. "It's a pleasure," is all he said. But it can't have been, putting up with all my whingeing and worries, my complaints and concerns.

"We should have a toast!" I declared. "To Anna and to Gwyn!"

"To Anna and Gwyn!" Stephen affirmed, raising his glass. New birth and new job, celebrated with as much panache as we could.

The sun sank a shade lower, catching the tree and throwing a shadow over my face. I gazed around at our home. The rains had destroyed the brightly-whitewashed walls that greeted me a year ago and the grass had hardly improved. Thomas and TomFum were sheltering under a leafy bush, contained by a low concrete-brick wall. All other plant life seemed to survive, although the shady garden inhibited the proliferation of colour.

In the shade of the mulberry tree

I leant back on the chair with my eyes closed. All I really wanted to do was sit here, in the company of my husband and children, and let Africa enfold me in its warmth. Here time slowed down. There was no doubting the patience required. Why do today what can be done tomorrow? The pace of life had infiltrated through my very being, such that I'd adopted the 'achieve one thing each day' motto. If I did it – great. If I did more – astonishing! If it didn't get done – well, did it really matter?

A thought struck me. "Ooh! We'll be able to see Anna when we go to the wedding in Ireland." I surprised myself with my excitement.

"It'll be great to be home, won't it," Stephen stated, sipping at his wine.

"Yes," I replied. It would be great to be home. But as I soaked up the remnants of the day's warmth, my mind was already planning for when we got back. The mosquito net needed to be hung above the spare bed and I would have to create more space for Gwyn, assuming she stayed with us for a while. Sherry and Precious required new uniforms and it would be great if we could get a decent irrigation system working in the garden. Matthew would move up a class, and by October I faced the prospect of Eleanor attending pre-school.

A cool evening breeze whispered to the mulberry tree above me. Already I was looking forward to coming home.

GLOSSARY

ABC	Abstain, Be faithful, use Condoms - the three-pronged attack against the spread of HIV/AIDS
braai	barbecue
EFZ	Evangelical Fellowship of Zambia
G&T	Gin & Tonic [drunk for medicinal purpose only, of course!]
GMA	Game Management Area
KNP	Kafue National Park
mukwa	local wood, dark hardwood streaked with lighter, weaker wood
mzungu	local term for white person, from the Swahili for 'aimless wanderer'
nshima	mealie meal: local staple food, mixed and cooked with water to the consistency of mashed potato
OVC	Orphans and Vulnerable Children
Paramount Chief	the tribal chief who is in charge of multiple chiefdoms in a region
rondavel	a round hut with a thatched roof
sms	"short message service" or text messaging on mobile (cell) phones
UTH	University Teaching Hospital
Zamtel	Zambia Telecommunications Company - supplier of telephone services
ZESCO	Zambia Electricity Supply Corporation Limited - electricity supplier

OTHER EXPLANATORY FACTS

Long distances are measured in kilometres, not miles. 1km = 0.625 miles.

Time is denoted entirely in the 24-hour clock, so meetings could be held, for example, at "10 hours" (10.00 am) or "16 hours" (4.00 pm). This magnificently avoids confusion over morning or evening timings.

Zambia has two seasons: dry (April to October) and wet (November to March). The cold 'winter' is June/July.

There are various different local languages but in the capital, Lusaka, the main one is Nyanja. Bemba is also widely spoken. However the official language is English.

On 1 January 2013 Zambia rebased the Zambian Kwacha, removing '000 from the currency.

RECOMMENDED READING:

The Africa House: The true story of an English Gentleman and his African dream, Christina Lamb, published by Viking Penguin

Catharine Withenay

Follow Catharine on Twitter
@c_withenay

www.facebook.com/CatharineWithenayWriter

www.catharinewithenay.com

Printed in Poland
by Amazon Fulfillment
Poland Sp. z o.o., Wrocław